Wisdom Of Chanakya

Timeless Lessons for Modern Life

Venkataraman Murali Ganesh

Wisdom of Chanakya
Timeless Lessons for Modern Life

Written by **Venkataraman Murali Ganesh**

First Edition: January 2025

For permission requests, write to the author at vmurali7465@gmail.com
[
ISBN: 978-93-341-9941-3

Self-Published by Author

DEDICATION

To my beloved parents, whose wisdom and values laid the foundation of my journey; to my wife, my pillar of strength, who inspires me with her unwavering love and encouragement; and to my children, my pride and joy, whose curiosity and dreams give purpose to all my endeavours.

This book is a testament to all you have taught and given me. Thank you for being my guiding light.

CONTENTS

Part 6: Timeless Lessons for Life

Summary

Appendices

Introduction

Who Was Chanakya?

Chapter 1

Chanakya, known as Kautilya or Vishnu Gupta, was a towering figure in ancient Indian history. Born around 371 BCE, he is celebrated as one of the most brilliant political strategists, economists, and philosophers ever. Chanakya's life and works are deeply intertwined with the foundation of the Mauryan Empire, which marked a pivotal era in Indian history. His intellectual contributions, notably the *Arthashastra*, a treatise on governance, economics, and statecraft, remain relevant even in modern times.

Early Life and Education

Chanakya was born in a humble Brahmin family in Takshashila (modern-day Taxila, Pakistan), a renowned learning centre during that period. He displayed remarkable intelligence from a young age and studied various disciplines, including philosophy, economics, politics, and military strategy. His education at Takshashila laid the foundation for his future as a master strategist and thinker.

Role in Establishing the Mauryan Empire

Chanakya's name is most famously associated with Chandragupta Maurya, the founder of the Mauryan Empire. Historical accounts suggest that Chanakya was crucial in mentoring and guiding Chandragupta to overthrow the Nanda dynasty, known for its corrupt and oppressive rule. Together, they established the Mauryan Empire, one of ancient India's most potent and well-administered empires.

The *Arthashastra*: His Magnum Opus

Chanakya's *Arthashastra* is a comprehensive statecraft, economics, and military strategy guide. It covers diverse topics such as governance, law, taxation, diplomacy, war, and ethics. The treatise reflects Chanakya's pragmatic approach to leadership, emphasising the need for a ruler to be shrewd, just, and visionary. His principles on governance, wealth management, and diplomacy have influenced not only ancient Indian rulers but also modern management and leadership practices.

Philosophical Beliefs and Teachings

Chanakya's philosophy was deeply rooted in realism and pragmatism. He believed that strong and ethical leadership, meticulous planning, and discipline were the cornerstone of a prosperous state. His teachings advocate self-reliance, strategic thinking, and a balanced personal and professional life approach. His quotes, such as "Before you start some work, always ask yourself three questions: Why am I doing it, what might the results be, and will I be successful?" continue to inspire individuals worldwide.

Legacy and Relevance

Chanakya's legacy transcends time and geography. His ideas on governance, economy, and ethics remain highly applicable today. Modern leaders, managers, and policymakers often draw parallels between Chanakya's teachings and contemporary challenges. His life exemplifies the power of knowledge, resilience, and strategic thinking in achieving greatness.

Chanakya was more than just a scholar; he was a visionary who understood the intricacies of human behaviour, power dynamics, and the art of leadership. His life and works serve as a timeless source of wisdom, offering lessons as relevant today as they were over two millennia ago.

The Relevance of Chanakya's Wisdom in Modern Times

Chapter 2

Chanakya's profound insights into governance, economics, leadership, and human behaviour have stood the test of time. Born over two millennia ago, his wisdom, encapsulated in works like the *Arthashastra* and the *Chanakya Neeti*, continues to inspire leaders, policymakers, and individuals across the globe. In today's fast-paced and complex world, Chanakya's teachings offer timeless solutions to contemporary challenges, making his philosophy as relevant as ever.

Leadership and Governance

One of Chanakya's central themes is the role of strong and ethical leadership in ensuring societal well-being. He emphasised that a leader must be wise, strategic, and deeply committed to the welfare of the people. This principle holds immense value in modern governance and corporate leadership, where decision-making often impacts millions of lives.

Modern Parallel: In today's political and business landscape, ethical leaders prioritising transparency, inclusivity, and long-term vision are paramount. Chanakya's advice to rulers—to be compassionate and pragmatic—provides a roadmap for building trust and fostering stability.

Economic Management

As the Arthashastra outlines, Chanakya's economic policies revolve around resource optimisation, taxation, trade, and wealth creation. He advocated for fair taxation, investment in infrastructure, and fostering trade relations to ensure a thriving economy.

Modern Parallel: Governments and businesses today can draw from Chanakya's insights to create sustainable economic systems. His emphasis on saving during prosperity to prepare for adversity aligns with contemporary financial planning and crisis management practices.

Strategic Thinking and Diplomacy

Chanakya was a master strategist who believed in meticulous planning and foresight. His diplomatic principles emphasised negotiation, alliances, and adaptability to achieve goals without unnecessary conflict.

Modern Parallel: In an era of globalisation and geopolitical challenges, Chanakya's teachings on diplomacy are invaluable. His strategies encourage collaboration, conflict resolution, and mutual benefit from international relations to corporate negotiations.

Human Resource Management

Chanakya recognised the importance of human capital and its role in building a prosperous state. He advised leaders to identify talent, nurture skills, and create an environment where individuals could contribute effectively to the larger goal.

Modern Parallel: This aligns closely with contemporary human resource practices, where employee engagement, skill development, and leadership training are key to organisational success. Chanakya's wisdom highlights the significance of empowering individuals to drive collective progress.

Ethics and Morality

While Chanakya's pragmatism is well-known, he also strongly emphasises ethics and dharma (righteousness). He believed that long-term success could only be achieved by adhering to principles of honesty and justice.

Modern Parallel: In a world increasingly grappling with ethical dilemmas, Chanakya's call for integrity in personal and professional life serves as a guiding light. His teachings remind us that short-term gains achieved through unethical means often lead to long-term instability.

Crisis Management

Chanakya's life and work reflect his ability to handle crises with composure and strategic thinking. His guidance to leaders during times of uncertainty emphasises preparation, adaptability, and resilience.

Modern Parallel: Whether it's navigating global pandemics, economic downturns, or organisational challenges, Chanakya's crisis management principles resonate deeply. His approach of anticipating challenges and building contingency plans is crucial in today's unpredictable world.

Personal Development

Chanakya's teachings extend beyond governance and economics to personal growth. He encouraged individuals to cultivate self-discipline, pursue knowledge, and maintain emotional intelligence. He famously said, "Education is the best friend. An educated person is respected everywhere. Education beats the beauty and the youth."

Modern Parallel: Personal development is a cornerstone of success today. Chanakya's emphasis on lifelong learning and self-improvement aligns with the modern focus on continuous skill enhancement and emotional well-being.

Summary

Chanakya's wisdom transcends time and geography, offering universally applicable lessons. His teachings on leadership, economics, strategy, and ethics provide a blueprint for navigating the complexities of modern life. In an era of rapid change and uncertainty, Chanakya's pragmatic yet principled approach is a source of inspiration and guidance.

By applying Chanakya's timeless lessons, individuals and organisations can foster resilience, innovation, and ethical progress. His legacy reminds us that true wisdom lies in understanding the nuances of human behaviour, preparing for the future, and balancing ambition with responsibility.

The Art of Balancing Tradition and Progress

Chapter 3

The interplay between tradition and progress is a delicate yet vital aspect of personal and societal growth. While traditions provide a culture's foundation and identity, progress drives innovation and adaptation. Chanakya, a visionary of his time, masterfully blended timeless principles with forward-thinking strategies. His teachings offer profound insights into achieving harmony between these seemingly contrasting forces.

Understanding Tradition: The Pillar of Stability

Tradition embodies the collective wisdom, values, and practices passed down through generations. It serves as a guiding light, offering a sense of identity and stability amidst changing times. Chanakya himself deeply respected the traditions of ancient India, recognising their role in fostering discipline, morality, and unity.

Lessons from Tradition:

- **Rooted Values:** Traditions provide a moral compass that helps individuals and societies make ethical decisions.
- **Sense of Belonging:** They create a shared identity and continuity, fostering social cohesion.
- **Resilience:** The enduring wisdom of traditions equips societies to navigate challenges and uncertainties.

Embracing Progress: The Engine of Growth

Progress, on the other hand, is the driving force that propels individuals and societies forward. It involves challenging old paradigms, embracing innovation, and adapting to evolving circumstances. Chanakya's visionary approach emphasised the importance of adapting traditional wisdom to meet contemporary needs.

Principles of Progress:

- **Innovation:** Progress thrives on creativity and the willingness to explore new possibilities.
- **Adaptability:** Embracing change ensures relevance in an ever-evolving world.
- **Growth Mindset:** Progress demands a focus on continuous learning and improvement.

Chanakya's Approach: The Perfect Balance

Chanakya's life and teachings exemplify the art of balancing tradition with progress. While he respected the foundational values of dharma (righteousness) and Niti (ethics), he also advocated for pragmatism and strategic thinking. His philosophy underscores that progress does not mean abandoning tradition but evolving it to remain relevant.

For instance, in his seminal work, the *Arthashastra*, Chanakya laid out administrative and economic principles rooted in ancient Indian wisdom while incorporating innovative strategies for governance, resource management, and diplomacy. This blend of tradition and progress created a robust framework for building and sustaining a mighty empire.

Lessons for Modern Times

In today's fast-paced world, balancing tradition and progress is more pertinent than ever. Businesses, governments, and individuals can draw inspiration from Chanakya's approach to creating sustainable and adaptable systems.

1. **Preserve Core Values:** While pursuing progress, it is essential to uphold core principles such as integrity, respect, and compassion.
2. **Leverage Technology:** Embrace technological advancements while ensuring they align with ethical and cultural norms.
3. **Foster Innovation within Frameworks:** Encourage creativity and innovation while respecting established guidelines and traditions.
4. **Promote Inclusive Growth:** Progress should benefit all sections of society, bridging gaps rather than creating divides.

Real-World Applications

- **In Leadership:** Leaders can uphold organisational values while driving innovation and adapting to market dynamics.
- **In Education:** Modern pedagogical tools and technologies can

complement traditional teaching methods.

- **In Lifestyle:** Individuals can adopt modern conveniences while cherishing cultural practices and rituals that enhance their identity and well-being.

Summary

The art of balancing tradition and progress lies in understanding that they are not opposing forces but complementary elements of growth. Traditions give us wisdom, while progress drives us toward a brighter future. Chanakya's teachings remind us that the most successful societies and individuals honour their past while boldly embracing change.

By harmonising the old with the new, we can create an innovative and grounded future, ensuring that our heritage's essence thrives alongside modernity's advancements.

Foundations of Leadership

Part 1

Leadership Qualities: Chanakya's Blueprint

Chapter 4

Chanakya, known as Kautilya, remains one of history's most revered strategists and thought leaders. His teachings on leadership, articulated in works like the *Arthashastra*, are as insightful today as they were over two millennia ago. According to Chanakya, effective leadership is not merely about authority but about understanding, strategy, and a deep commitment to the welfare of one's people. His principles offer a timeless blueprint for cultivating leadership qualities that resonate personally and professionally.

1. Visionary Thinking

Chanakya believed that a leader must possess a clear and long-term vision. A leader's ability to foresee challenges, opportunities, and trends is crucial for guiding their team or organisation towards success. He advised leaders to plan meticulously and prepare for unforeseen circumstances.

Modern Application: Leaders today must anticipate market shifts, technological advancements, and societal changes to steer their organisations effectively. Visionary thinking enables them to set goals that inspire and motivate others.

2. Ethical Conduct and Integrity

Ethics and integrity form the cornerstone of leadership in Chanakya's philosophy. He emphasised that a leader's actions should reflect moral principles and a commitment to justice. A leader who upholds ethics earns the trust and respect of their followers.

Modern Application: Transparency, accountability, and fairness are indispensable in today's leadership landscape. Ethical leadership fosters trust, enhances reputation, and creates a positive organisational culture.

3. Emotional Intelligence

Chanakya recognised the importance of understanding human emotions and behaviour. He advised leaders to be empathetic, adaptable, and tactful in their interactions with others. Leaders can inspire loyalty and commitment by connecting with people on an emotional level.

Modern Application: Emotional intelligence—the ability to understand and manage one's emotions while empathising with others—is a critical leadership skill. It helps resolve conflicts, build strong teams, and foster collaboration.

4. Decisiveness

One of Chanakya's key teachings is the importance of decisiveness. He believed a leader should analyse situations thoroughly but act swiftly when necessary. Indecision, he argued, can lead to missed opportunities and weakened authority.

Modern Application: Leaders in fast-paced environments must make informed decisions promptly. Decisiveness instils confidence in the team and ensures progress, even in challenging situations.

5. Strategic Thinking

Chanakya's *Arthashastra* is a testament to his unparalleled strategic acumen. He taught that leaders must plan, consider all possible outcomes, and devise strategies that align with their goals. Strategic thinking involves balancing short-term needs with long-term objectives.

Modern Application: In today's competitive world, leaders must adopt a strategic mindset to navigate complexities, mitigate risks, and capitalise on opportunities. A well-thought-out strategy can be the difference between success and failure.

6. Self-Discipline and Resilience

Chanakya believed that leaders must first lead themselves before leading others. Great leaders are defined by self-discipline, resilience, and the ability to remain focused under pressure. He also stressed the importance of continual self-improvement.

Modern Application: Leaders who practice self-discipline inspire their teams through example. Resilience in adversity ensures they can navigate challenges and motivate others to do the same.

7. Empowerment and Delegation

Chanakya taught that a wise leader empowers their team by recognising individual strengths and delegating responsibilities effectively. Trusting others to carry out tasks fosters a sense of ownership and accountability.

Modern Application: Modern leaders who empower their teams create an environment of collaboration and innovation. Delegation not only optimises productivity but also cultivates future leaders within the organisation.

8. Communication Skills

Clear and effective communication was a hallmark of Chanakya's leadership teachings. He believed leaders must clearly articulate their vision, goals, and expectations to ensure alignment and unity.

Modern Application: In the digital age, communication skills are more critical than ever. Leaders must convey ideas persuasively, listen actively, and engage with diverse stakeholders across multiple platforms.

9. Adaptability and Innovation

Chanakya's strategies often involved adapting to changing circumstances and embracing innovative solutions. He emphasised the need for flexibility in thought and action to stay relevant in a dynamic environment.

Modern Application: Leaders today must be open to change and willing to explore new approaches. Adaptability ensures they can pivot strategies as needed, while innovation drives progress and differentiation.

10. Commitment to the Greater Good

Chanakya's ultimate goal was the welfare of the state and its people. He taught that a true leader's success lies in uplifting others and creating a lasting positive impact.

Modern Application: Socially responsible leadership prioritising sustainability, inclusivity, and community welfare is increasingly valued. Leaders who align their goals with the greater good inspire trust and loyalty.

Summary

Chanakya's leadership blueprint remains a beacon of wisdom for leaders across generations. His emphasis on vision, ethics, strategy, and resilience offers practical lessons for navigating the complexities of leadership in modern times. By integrating these timeless principles into their approach, today's leaders can inspire transformation, achieve meaningful goals, and leave a legacy of positive change.

Visionary Thinking and Strategic Planning

Chapter 5

Visionary thinking and strategic planning are cornerstones of effective leadership and governance, principles that Chanakya emphasised throughout his teachings. These concepts are as vital today as they were in his time, guiding individuals and organisations to anticipate challenges, seize opportunities, and achieve long-term success.

The Essence of Visionary Thinking

Visionary thinking involves the ability to foresee future possibilities and trends. It is about imagining a better future and setting the direction to achieve it. Chanakya's visionary approach enabled him to see beyond immediate concerns and devise strategies that shaped the destiny of entire kingdoms.

Key Attributes of Visionary Thinking:

1. **Foresight:** The ability to anticipate potential scenarios and prepare accordingly.
2. **Creativity:** Thinking beyond conventional boundaries to envision innovative solutions.
3. **Purpose-driven:** Establishing goals that align with a greater mission or objective.
4. **Adaptability:** Recognising that visions may evolve and require recalibration in response to changing circumstances.

Chanakya's Visionary Leadership

Chanakya's life offers numerous examples of his visionary thinking. One of his most notable achievements was uniting fragmented Indian kingdoms to establish the Mauryan Empire. He envisioned a unified and powerful state capable of resisting external threats and fostering prosperity. To realise this vision, he cultivated leaders, developed alliances, and meticulously planned for the long-term stability of the empire.

Strategic Planning: The Roadmap to Vision

While visionary thinking defines the destination, strategic planning is the roadmap. Chanakya's *Arthashastra* is a comprehensive strategic planning manual offering insights into governance, economics, military strategy, and diplomacy. His emphasis on detailed planning and execution underscores the importance of aligning short-term actions with long-term goals.

Elements of Strategic Planning:

1. **Assessment:** Analysing strengths, weaknesses, opportunities, and threats (SWOT).
2. **Prioritisation:** Identifying critical objectives and focusing resources on achieving them.
3. **Resource Management:** Ensuring optimal financial, human, and material asset utilisation.
4. **Execution:** Implementing plans with precision and accountability.
5. **Evaluation:** Continuously monitoring progress and adjusting strategies as needed.

Modern Applications of Chanakya's Teachings

1. **Corporate Leadership:** Visionary corporate leaders use Chanakya's principles to anticipate market trends, innovate products, and build sustainable organisations. Strategic planning enables them to manage resources effectively, outmanoeuvre competitors, and achieve long-term profitability.
2. **Government and Public Policy:** Policymakers can draw inspiration from Chanakya's foresight and planning to design policies that address contemporary challenges such as climate change, economic inequality, and public health crises.
3. **Personal Growth:** Individuals can apply visionary thinking and strategic planning to set and achieve personal and professional goals. By envisioning their ideal future and crafting actionable steps, they can navigate life's complexities with purpose and confidence.

Balancing Vision and Strategy

Chanakya's wisdom underscores the importance of balancing vision and strategy. Vision without action remains a dream, and action without vision leads to chaos. Successful leaders harmonise these elements to inspire others, foster innovation, and create lasting impact.

Summary

Visionary thinking and strategic planning are timeless skills that define great leaders and organisations. By embracing Chanakya's principles, we can learn to think beyond immediate challenges, craft actionable roadmaps, and navigate the complexities of the modern world. His teachings remind us that a clear vision and meticulous planning are the key to achieving extraordinary success and leaving a legacy that endures.

The Role of Ethics in Leadership

Chapter 6

Ethics form the backbone of effective and sustainable leadership. A leader's decisions and actions influence immediate outcomes and set the tone for the values and culture of their organisation or community. Chanakya's teachings underscore the indispensable role of ethics in leadership, emphasising that the accurate measure of a leader lies in their adherence to principles of righteousness and justice.

Ethics: The Foundation of Leadership

Ethics in leadership refers to the moral principles and values that guide a leader's behaviour and decisions. They ensure that power is exercised responsibly and in the best interest of others. Chanakya's leadership philosophy is rooted in dharma, a commitment to righteousness and the greater good.

Core Ethical Principles for Leaders:

1. **Integrity:** Staying true to one's values and commitments.
2. **Accountability:** Taking responsibility for one's actions and their consequences.
3. **Fairness:** Treating everyone with impartiality and justice.
4. **Transparency:** Maintaining openness in decision-making processes.
5. **Empathy:** Considering the needs and perspectives of others.

Chanakya's Ethical Leadership Philosophy

Chanakya believed that ethics and leadership are inseparable. He advocated for leaders who prioritise the welfare of their people over personal gain. His teachings stress that unethical behaviour, while it may yield short-term gains, ultimately leads to instability and failure.

Key Teachings on Ethical Leadership:

- **Righteous Governance:** A ruler's primary duty is to ensure justice and fairness for all. - **Moral Authority:** Ethical leaders earn the trust and loyalty of their followers, creating a stable and harmonious environment.

- **Long-Term Vision:** Ethical decisions may require sacrifices but pave the way for sustainable success.

The Modern Relevance of Ethical Leadership

In today's world, ethical leadership is more critical than ever. Rapid globalisation, technological advancements, and increasing social awareness demand leaders who act with integrity and responsibility. Organisations led by ethical leaders tend to foster trust, attract talent, and build enduring reputations.

Applications of Ethical Leadership:

1. **Corporate Leadership:** Ethical leaders in business prioritise stakeholder interests, ensuring fair practices and social responsibility.
2. **Public Administration:** Governments must adopt transparent and accountable practices to maintain public trust.
3. **Community Leadership:** Leaders in local and social contexts can inspire change by upholding ethical values.

Balancing Power and Morality

One of the most significant challenges for leaders is balancing the exercise of power with moral responsibility. Chanakya's teachings provide valuable insights into achieving this balance:

- **Avoid Corruption:** Leaders must resist using power for personal benefit.
- **Lead by Example:** Ethical behaviour at the top sets a standard for the organisation.
- **Seek Counsel:** Wise advisors can help leaders make decisions that align with ethical standards.

Challenges in Ethical Leadership

While the benefits of ethical leadership are clear, practising it is not without challenges. Leaders may face dilemmas where ethical choices conflict with practical or immediate gains. Chanakya's teachings remind us that enduring success often requires prioritising principles over convenience.

Overcoming Challenges:

- Develop a clear code of ethics as a guide for decision-making.
- Foster a culture that values and rewards ethical behaviour.
- Stay committed to self-reflection and continual improvement.

Summary

Ethics are the cornerstone of leadership, inspiring trust, loyalty, and sustainable success. Chanakya's wisdom highlights the timeless importance of ethical conduct in leadership, reminding us that authentic leadership is not just about achieving goals but about how those goals are achieved. By prioritising integrity, fairness, and responsibility, leaders can create a legacy of positive impact and lasting change.

Decision-Making: Balancing Emotion and Logic

Chapter 7

Decision-making is one of the most critical aspects of leadership and governance. The ability to make sound decisions often determines the success or failure of leaders, organisations, and even nations. Chanakya's teachings emphasise a balanced approach to decision-making—one that integrates emotional intelligence and logical reasoning.

The Dual Facets of Decision-Making

Chanakya recognised that human decisions are influenced by two powerful forces: emotion and logic. While emotions bring empathy and human connection to decisions, logic ensures rationality and objectivity. A balanced approach combines both strengths, leading to effective, fair, and sustainable outcomes.

Emotion in Decision-Making:

1. Builds trust and empathy.
2. Considers the human impact of decisions.
3. Encourages compassion and inclusivity.

Logic in Decision-Making:

1. Ensures rationality and objectivity.
2. Focuses on data and evidence.
3. Evaluate long-term consequences.

Chanakya's Philosophy on Decision-Making

Chanakya's *Arthashastra* offers profound insights into decision-making. He advocated for leaders to remain calm and composed, avoiding impulsive decisions driven solely by emotions. At the same time, he cautioned against cold, detached logic that disregards human needs and relationships.

Key Teachings:

- **Weigh All Factors:** Evaluate the pros and cons of every decision.
- **Stay Detached but Compassionate:** Avoid becoming emotionally entangled but empathise with those affected.
- **Consult Wisely:** Seek advice from knowledgeable and impartial advisors to gain diverse perspectives.

Balancing Emotion and Logic: Practical Steps

1. **Pause Before Acting:** Reflect, especially in emotionally charged situations. This pause allows for a clearer perspective and prevents hasty decisions.
2. **Gather Information:** Use logic to analyse data and facts. Ensure that evidence rather than assumptions back decisions.
3. **Consider Human Impact:** Evaluate how decisions affect individuals and communities. Emotional intelligence helps in understanding and addressing these impacts.
4. **Seek Counsel:** Surround yourself with advisors who can provide analytical insights and empathetic viewpoints.
5. **Use a Structured Framework:** Develop a decision-making process incorporating emotional and logical considerations. For example:
    - Define the problem clearly.
    - Gather data and input from stakeholders.
    - Consider potential outcomes, both tangible and intangible.
    - Make a decision and communicate it effectively.

Modern Applications of Chanakya's Wisdom

1. In Business: Corporate leaders face complex decisions that impact employees, shareholders, and customers. A balance of emotion and logic ensures profitability while maintaining ethical and socially responsible practices.

2. In Politics: Policymakers must consider the immediate needs of citizens alongside long-term national interests. Decisions driven by empathy for the public yet grounded in sound analysis yield sustainable outcomes.

3. In Personal Life: Chanakya's principles can help individuals navigate personal and professional dilemmas. Balancing heart and mind enables more fulfilling relationships and better career choices.

Overcoming Common Pitfalls

1. **Emotional Overload:** Decisions driven purely by emotion can lead to favouritism, irrationality, or unintended consequences. To overcome this, step back and assess the situation with objectivity.

2. **Over-Reliance on Logic:** Excessive focus on logic can lead to cold, impersonal decisions that alienate others. Cultivate empathy to ensure your choices resonate with those affected.
3. **Fear of Mistakes:** Indecision often arises from fear of failure. Chanakya advised leaders to embrace calculated risks and learn from mistakes rather than being paralysed.

Chanakya's Timeless Insight

"Before you start work, ask yourself three questions: Why am I doing it? What might the results be? Will I be successful?" This quote encapsulates the essence of balancing emotion and logic. Asking "why" invokes empathy and purpose, while "what" and "will" engage critical thinking and planning.

Summary

Decision-making is both an art and a science. Chanakya's wisdom teaches us that neither emotion nor logic alone is sufficient; true mastery lies in harmonising the two. Leaders who embrace this balanced approach can make decisions that are not only effective but also ethical and inclusive. By applying Chanakya's principles, we can navigate the complexities of modern life with clarity, compassion, and confidence.

Personal Development

Part 2

Self-Discipline: The Core of Success

Chapter 8

Self-discipline is the foundation upon which all outstanding achievements are built. Chanakya, one of the most brilliant minds in Indian history, placed immense importance on self-discipline as a critical quality for individuals seeking success in personal and professional life. His teachings emphasise that controlling one's impulses and staying focused on long-term goals is a hallmark of a strong and capable leader.

The Meaning of Self-Discipline

Self-discipline is regulating and controlling one's emotions, thoughts, and behaviours to pursue a goal. It involves making decisions that align with one's values and objectives, even in the face of distractions, challenges, or temptations.

Key Elements of Self-Discipline:

1. **Focus:** Concentrating on priorities and avoiding distractions.
2. **Consistency:** Persisting in actions and habits that lead to success.
3. **Self-Control:** Managing emotions and impulses effectively.
4. **Accountability:** Taking responsibility for one's actions and decisions.

Chanakya's Perspective on Self-Discipline

Chanakya's life and teachings exemplify self-discipline. As the architect of the Mauryan Empire, he demonstrated remarkable focus and perseverance in achieving his vision of a united and prosperous India. In his seminal work, *Arthashastra*, Chanakya outlined the importance of disciplined leadership and governance.

Notable Teachings on Self-Discipline:

- "Before you conquer the world, you must conquer yourself." This reflects the belief that self-discipline is a prerequisite for any external success.
- Chanakya emphasised the need for leaders to maintain discipline in

thought, action, and speech to inspire trust and respect among their followers.

The Role of Self-Discipline in Success

Self-discipline is the driving force behind consistent effort and resilience, two essential qualities for success. Without discipline, even the most talented individuals may falter in adversity.

Benefits of Self-Discipline:

1. **Enhanced Productivity:** Staying focused on tasks leads to efficient use of time and resources.
2. **Stronger Willpower:** Resisting distractions and temptations fosters resilience.
3. **Improved Decision-Making:** Disciplined individuals are likelier to make thoughtful and informed choices.
4. **Achievement of Goals:** Consistent effort and perseverance result in tangible progress.

Practical Strategies for Cultivating Self-Discipline

1. **Set Clear Goals:** Define specific, measurable, and time-bound objectives to stay focused.
2. **Develop Daily Habits:** Establish routines that align with your goals, such as regular exercise, reading, or planning.
3. **Practice Delayed Gratification:** Prioritise long-term benefits over immediate pleasures.
4. **Monitor Progress:** Regularly evaluate your actions and adjust to stay on track.
5. **Stay Accountable:** Share your goals with a trusted friend or mentor who can hold you accountable.

Modern Applications of Chanakya's Teachings

1. **In Leadership:** Leaders who practice self-discipline set an example for their teams, fostering a culture of commitment and excellence.
2. **In Education:** Students who develop disciplined study habits are better equipped to succeed academically.
3. **In Personal Growth:** Self-discipline enables individuals to break bad habits, cultivate positive behaviours, and achieve their potential.

Challenges and Overcoming Them

Common Obstacles:

- **Procrastination:** Delaying tasks due to lack of motivation or fear of failure.
- **Distractions:** The lure of entertainment, social media, or other non-essential activities.
- **Inconsistency:** Difficulty maintaining routines and habits over time.

Solutions:

- Break tasks into smaller, manageable steps to reduce overwhelm.
- Use tools like time-blocking or apps to minimise distractions.
- Celebrate small victories to maintain motivation and momentum.

Chanakya's Wisdom for Today's World

Chanakya's emphasis on self-discipline remains highly relevant in today's fast-paced and distraction-filled world. His teachings encourage us to:

- Stay grounded in our values amidst external pressures.
- Focus on meaningful goals rather than fleeting pleasures.
- Develop the resilience needed to navigate challenges and setbacks.

Summary

Self-discipline is not just a trait but a way of life that enables individuals to unlock their full potential. Chanakya's wisdom is a timeless guide, reminding us that the path to success is paved with consistency, focus, and perseverance. By cultivating self-discipline, we can achieve greatness and leave a lasting impact on the world.

The Power of Knowledge and Continuous Learning

Chapter 9

Knowledge is the cornerstone of human progress and success. It equips individuals with the tools to understand, innovate, and adapt in an ever-changing world. Chanakya, a luminary of ancient India, profoundly understood the value of knowledge and lifelong learning. He emphasised that true power lies not in wealth or position but wisdom and the continuous pursuit of education.

Chanakya's Philosophy on Knowledge

Chanakya's writings and teachings, especially in the *Arthashastra* and *Chanakya Niti*, repeatedly highlight the transformative power of knowledge. For him, knowledge was a treasure that could not be stolen, a force that elevated individuals and nations alike.

Notable Teachings:

- "Knowledge is your greatest friend. It stays with you even when everything else is lost."
- He advocated for leaders and citizens to invest in education to achieve personal and societal growth.

Why Knowledge Matters

1. **Empowerment:** Knowledge empowers individuals to make informed decisions and seize opportunities.
2. **Innovation** fosters creativity and the ability to solve complex problems.
3. **Adaptability:** A well-informed mind can navigate challenges and changes better.
4. **Leadership:** Knowledgeable leaders inspire trust and are better equipped to guide their communities or organisations.

The Need for Continuous Learning

In a rapidly evolving world, resting on past knowledge is insufficient. Continuous learning ensures that individuals and organisations remain relevant and competitive.

Benefits of Continuous Learning:

1. **Keeps Skills Current:** Learning new skills and technologies ensures adaptability in dynamic environments.
2. **Enhances Critical Thinking:** Exposure to diverse ideas fosters better analysis and decision-making.
3. **Drives Personal Growth:** Continuous learning cultivates confidence and broadens perspectives.
4. **Promotes Innovation:** Staying curious leads to new ideas and creative solutions.

Modern Applications of Chanakya's Wisdom

1. **In Professional Life:**
    - Organisations thrive when employees invest in upskilling. Training programs and certifications are essential for staying ahead.
    - Leaders who prioritise learning set a culture of growth within their teams.
2. **In Personal Life:**
    - Reading, taking courses, or engaging in discussions sharpens intellect and enriches life experiences.
    - Hobbies and interests outside one's profession also contribute to holistic development.
3. **In Education:**
    - Chanakya's emphasis on education can inspire policymakers to invest in accessible and quality education systems.
    - Encouraging curiosity from a young age ensures a lifelong habit of learning.

How to Cultivate Continuous Learning

1. **Adopt a Growth Mindset:** Belief in the potential to improve through effort and perseverance.
2. **Set Learning Goals:** Define clear objectives for what you want to learn and why.
3. **Leverage Technology:** Stay updated with online courses, webinars, and resources.

4. **Seek Mentorship:** Learn from experts and peers who can guide and challenge you.
5. **Reflect and Apply:** Regularly reflect on what you've learned and find ways to apply it in real-life situations.

Overcoming Barriers to Learning

1. **Lack of Time:** Prioritise learning by setting aside dedicated time each day or week.
2. **Fear of Failure:** Embrace mistakes as opportunities to grow.
3. **Complacency:** Stay curious and motivated by connecting learning goals to personal or professional aspirations.
4. **Resource Limitations:** Utilise free or low-cost learning platforms and libraries.

Chanakya's Eternal Insight

Chanakya's wisdom underscores the timeless relevance of knowledge and learning. He believed that an educated and informed society is the bedrock of a strong and prosperous nation. His teachings remind us that pursuing knowledge is not a destination but a lifelong journey.
"Just as a tree laden with fruits bows down, a truly learned person is humble." This quote reflects the essence of continuous learning—the more we learn, the more we realise how much there is to know.

Summary

The power of knowledge and continuous learning lies in its ability to transform individuals, organisations, and societies. Chanakya's emphasis on education and lifelong learning is as relevant today as it was centuries ago. By embracing his teachings, we can unlock our potential, drive innovation, and build a future rooted in wisdom and understanding. As Chanakya demonstrated, knowledge is the path to enduring success.

Emotional Intelligence: Lessons from Chanakya's Teachings

Chapter 10

Emotional intelligence—understanding, managing, and harnessing emotions—is a cornerstone of effective leadership and interpersonal relationships. Chanakya, the legendary strategist and thinker, recognised the importance of emotional mastery in achieving personal and professional success. His teachings, rooted in observation and experience, offer timeless insights into the value of emotional intelligence in decision-making, leadership, and navigating complex social dynamics.

Chanakya's Perspective on Emotions

Chanakya's writings underscore the importance of controlling one's emotions and using them wisely. He believed unchecked emotions could lead to impulsive decisions, while disciplined emotions could foster clarity and wisdom.

Key Teachings:

- "The wise do not reveal their emotions in haste; they analyse the situation and act accordingly." This highlights the importance of emotional regulation and thoughtful responses.
- Chanakya emphasised self-awareness as the first step in understanding and managing emotions effectively.

Core Components of Emotional Intelligence

1. **Self-awareness:** Understanding your emotions and how they influence your thoughts and actions.
    - Chanakya's focus on introspection aligns with the modern concept of self-awareness. He advocated regular self-reflection to identify strengths, weaknesses, and emotional triggers.

2. **Self-Regulation:** The ability to control impulsive behaviours and respond appropriately.
    - o Chanakya's advice to leaders often included strategies for remaining calm under pressure and avoiding decisions made in anger or haste.
3. **Empathy:** The capacity to understand and share the feelings of others.
    - o Chanakya stressed the importance of understanding the emotions and motivations of others to build trust and rapport.
4. **Social Skills:** Managing relationships and influencing others effectively.
    - o His diplomacy and conflict resolution strategies underscore the importance of clear communication and mutual respect.
5. **Motivation:** Harnessing emotions to stay focused on goals.
    - o Chanakya's life is a testament to perseverance and the ability to channel emotions into constructive action.

Applying Chanakya's Wisdom to Emotional Intelligence

1. **Mastering Self-Control:**
    - o Chanakya's teachings often emphasise the dangers of anger and impulsivity. Leaders and individuals must learn to pause, reflect, and choose their responses wisely.
    - o Practice mindfulness techniques to remain grounded in emotionally charged situations.
2. **Cultivating Empathy:**
    - o "Understanding the emotions of others is as important as understanding your own." Chanakya's approach to governance and strategy often involved putting himself in the shoes of his adversaries or allies.
    - o Actively listen to others and validate their feelings to foster stronger connections.
3. **Balancing Emotion and Logic:**
    - o Chanakya's strategies were a blend of emotional intelligence and sharp intellect. He encouraged weighing emotional responses against logical reasoning to make sound decisions.
    - o Develop critical thinking skills to evaluate situations from multiple perspectives.
4. **Building Resilience:**
    - o Chanakya's life was filled with setbacks, yet his perseverance reflects emotional strength and resilience.
    - o Practice gratitude and focus on solutions to build emotional endurance.

5. **Effective Communication:**
    - Chanakya's diplomatic skills highlight the role of clear, respectful communication in resolving conflicts and building alliances.
    - Use emotional intelligence to tailor your communication style to the needs and emotions of your audience.

Modern Relevance of Chanakya's Teachings

1. **In Leadership:**
    - Leaders who embody emotional intelligence inspire trust, motivate teams, and navigate crises effectively.
    - Chanakya's emphasis on empathy and self-regulation guides modern leaders aiming to balance authority with approachability.
2. **In Relationships:**
    - Emotional intelligence fosters healthier relationships by enhancing understanding and reducing conflicts.
    - Chanakya's advice to build trust and avoid deceit applies to personal and professional interactions.
3. **In Personal Growth:**
    - Continuous self-reflection and emotional management enable individuals to achieve their goals and maintain mental well-being.
    - Chanakya's call for introspection remains a timeless tool for personal development.

Challenges in Developing Emotional Intelligence

1. **Emotional Reactivity:** Impulsive reactions can hinder relationships and decision-making.
    - Solution: Practice deep breathing and mindfulness to pause before responding.
2. **Lack of Empathy:** Difficulty understanding others' emotions can lead to miscommunication.
    - Solution: Engage in active listening and seek diverse perspectives.
3. **Resistance to Feedback:** Avoiding constructive criticism can stall growth.
    - Solution: Embrace feedback as an opportunity to learn and improve.

Chanakya's Eternal Wisdom

Chanakya's teachings on emotional intelligence remind us of the power of emotional mastery in achieving success and harmony. His emphasis on self-awareness, empathy, and resilience resonates today, where emotional intelligence is critical in leadership and personal life.

Summary

Emotional intelligence is not an innate trait but a skill that can be cultivated through practice and reflection. Chanakya's wisdom provides a timeless framework for mastering emotions and building meaningful relationships. Integrating his teachings into our lives allows us to balance emotion and logic, foster empathy, and lead with integrity. As Chanakya demonstrated, emotional intelligence is a pathway to enduring success and harmony in life.

Cultivating Resilience and Self-Reliance

Chapter 11

Resilience and self-reliance are fundamental traits for navigating life's uncertainties and challenges. These qualities empower individuals to recover from setbacks, adapt to change, and confidently chart their course. Chanakya, a master strategist and philosopher, offered profound insights into building resilience and fostering self-reliance. His teachings remain timeless, guiding individuals striving to overcome adversity and achieve independence.

Chanakya's Philosophy on Resilience

Chanakya's life itself was a testament to resilience. Despite facing personal and political upheavals, he emerged as a key figure in shaping the Mauryan Empire. His writings emphasise the importance of inner strength and the ability to withstand adversity without losing focus on one's goals.

Key Teachings:

- "A man is great not because he hasn't fallen but because he rises every time he falls." This reflects the essence of resilience—perseverance despite difficulties.
- Chanakya advocated for learning from failures and using them as stepping stones for success.

The Role of Self-Reliance

For Chanakya, self-reliance was a cornerstone of personal and societal progress. He believed that true independence comes from the ability to rely on one's efforts, skills, and judgment.

Key Teachings:

- "One who is self-dependent earns respect and lives with dignity."
- He encouraged individuals to cultivate skills and knowledge to become self-sufficient.

Building Resilience: Lessons from Chanakya

1. **Develop a Strong Mindset:**
   - Chanakya emphasised the importance of mental fortitude in overcoming challenges.
   - Practice mindfulness and positive affirmations to build mental strength.

2. **Learn from Adversity:**
   - Failures and hardships are growth opportunities.
   - Reflect on setbacks to identify lessons and strategies for future success.

3. **Adapt to Change:**
   - Flexibility is key to resilience. Chanakya's strategies often involved adapting to changing political and social landscapes.
   - Cultivate a mindset that embraces change as an opportunity rather than a threat.

4. **Maintain Long-Term Vision:**
   - Chanakya's strategic planning was rooted in a clear vision for the future.
   - Set long-term goals and remain focused, even during temporary setbacks.

5. **Build a Support System:**
   - Resilience is strengthened through connections. Chanakya understood the importance of alliances in achieving larger goals.
   - Foster relationships with mentors, peers, and loved ones who can provide guidance and encouragement.

Fostering Self-Reliance: Lessons from Chanakya

1. **Cultivate Knowledge and Skills:**
   - Knowledge is the foundation of independence. Chanakya's emphasis on education underscores its role in self-reliance.
   - Continuously learn and upgrade your skills to remain relevant

and capable.

2. **Practice Financial Discipline:**
    - Financial independence is a critical aspect of self-reliance. Chanakya's teachings on wealth management highlight the importance of saving and prudent investment.
    - Create a budget, save regularly, and avoid unnecessary debts.

3. **Trust Your Abilities:**
    - Self-confidence is essential for self-reliance. Chanakya's life shows how belief in one's capabilities can lead to monumental achievements.
    - Focus on your strengths and work on areas of improvement.

4. **Plan for Contingencies:**
    - Chanakya's strategies always included preparation for unforeseen circumstances.
    - Build an emergency fund and have alternative plans to mitigate risks.

5. **Embrace Responsibility:**
    - Self-reliance grows when individuals take ownership of their actions and decisions.
    - Be proactive in solving problems rather than waiting for external help.

Modern Relevance of Chanakya's Teachings

1. **In Professional Life:**
    - Resilience helps employees and entrepreneurs overcome workplace challenges and uncertainties.
    - Self-reliance fosters innovation and independence, enabling individuals to excel in their careers.

2. **In Personal Life:**
   - Resilience helps individuals navigate personal setbacks such as loss or failure.
   - Self-reliance builds confidence and reduces dependency on others for happiness or success.

3. **In Society:**
   - A resilient and self-reliant population contributes to a nation's strength and prosperity.
   - Chanakya's emphasis on education and skill development can inspire policies that promote self-sufficiency.

Practical Steps to Cultivate Resilience and Self-Reliance

1. **Set Realistic Goals:** Break larger objectives into manageable steps to avoid overwhelm.
2. **Celebrate Progress:** Acknowledge small victories to stay motivated.
3. **Stay Optimistic:** Focus on possibilities rather than obstacles.
4. **Invest in Yourself:** Prioritise personal growth through learning, health, and self-care.
5. **Take Calculated Risks:** Embrace challenges that push you out of your comfort zone.

Chanakya's Enduring Insight

"He who depends on himself will attain the greatest happiness." This wisdom underscores the essence of resilience and self-reliance. By cultivating these traits, individuals can navigate life's complexities with courage and clarity.

Summary

Chanakya's teachings on resilience and self-reliance offer a timeless blueprint for overcoming adversity and achieving independence. These qualities are more crucial than ever in today's fast-paced and unpredictable world. By embracing his wisdom, individuals can build the strength and confidence to thrive in all aspects of life, transforming challenges into opportunities for growth.

Governance and Management

Part 3

Chanakya's Principles of Good Governance

Chapter 12

Chanakya, known as Kautilya, remains one of history's most significant political thinkers and strategists. His magnum opus, the *Arthashastra*, provides timeless principles of governance that have influenced leaders for centuries. Chanakya's vision of good governance was rooted in ethics, practical wisdom, and the welfare of the state and its people. Here, we explore the core principles of governance as envisioned by Chanakya:

---

1. The Welfare of the People is Paramount

Chanakya asserted that the ruler's happiness lies in the people's happiness. He famously stated:

"In the happiness of his subjects lies the king's happiness; in their welfare lies his welfare."

A leader must prioritise the well-being of citizens over personal ambition or wealth. This principle emphasises that governance should focus on creating prosperity, safety, and justice for all.

---

2. Leadership by Example

Chanakya believed that a leader must set high standards of conduct and integrity. He wrote:

"As the leader, so the followers."

A ruler who practices self-discipline, fairness, and accountability inspires the same qualities in their administration and citizens. Leadership by example builds trust and respect.

---

3. Ethical Governance

Ethics and morality formed the backbone of Chanakya's governance model.

While he advocated pragmatism, he stressed that actions must not violate the ethical fabric of society. He believed that:

"The power of ethical conduct is greater than that of arms."

Governments that adhere to ethical principles gain the loyalty and support of their people.

---

4. Strategic Planning and Foresight

A successful ruler must plan strategically, anticipate challenges, and adapt to changing circumstances. Chanakya's principles emphasised:

- Assessing risks and opportunities.
- Preparing for future crises.
- Maintaining a long-term vision for the state's development.

His advice remains relevant for modern leaders navigating complex political and economic landscapes.

---

5. Administration and Bureaucracy

Chanakya recognised the importance of an efficient administrative system.

He advocated for:

- Appointing qualified and loyal officials.
- Regularly monitoring and evaluating the performance of administrators.
- Eliminating corruption and inefficiency.

"The ruler who provides justice and fairness ensures the stability of his kingdom."

---

6. Rule of Law

Chanakya emphasised the supremacy of law over the whims of rulers. A strong legal framework was essential for maintaining order and ensuring justice.

His principles on law included:

- Fair trials and impartiality in judgment.
- Strict enforcement of rules to prevent chaos.
- Protecting the rights and duties of every individual.

7. Economic Stability

A prosperous economy was central to Chanakya's vision of good governance. He wrote extensively on:

- Encouraging trade and agriculture.
- Implementing fair taxation policies.
- Managing state finances with prudence.

A strong economy, he argued, supports a stable and secure state.

8. Défense and Security

Chanakya viewed security as a vital pillar of governance. He proposed measures to:

- Maintain a strong and well-trained army.
- Protect borders and internal stability.
- Use diplomacy, alliances, and intelligence to safeguard the state.

"A ruler who fails to defend his kingdom will see its downfall."

9. Diplomacy and International Relations

Chanakya was a Master of Diplomacy. He advised rulers to:

- Build strategic alliances.
- Use negotiation and compromise to resolve conflicts.
- Maintain vigilance against potential adversaries.

His six-fold foreign relations policy—peace, war, neutrality, alliance, double policy, and seeking shelter—remains a cornerstone of international strategy.

10. Adaptability and Pragmatism

Chanakya emphasised the need for rulers to adapt to changing circumstances without compromising core principles. He encouraged pragmatism in decision-making and recognised that:

"One must bend with the wind to prevent breaking."

Flexibility ensures the longevity of leadership and institutions.

11. Education and Knowledge

Chanakya highlighted the importance of education for both rulers and citizens. A knowledgeable ruler could make informed decisions, and an educated populace could contribute to the state's progress. He believed:

"Knowledge is power and the foundation of all success."

---

12. Resilience and Crisis Management

Governance, according to Chanakya, requires resilience in the face of adversity. He advised leaders to remain calm, act decisively, and inspire confidence during crises.

His teachings on crisis management include:

- Anticipating potential threats.
- Preparing contingency plans.
- Leading with courage and resolve.

Summary

Chanakya's principles of good governance are a testament to his understanding of human nature, society, and statecraft. His teachings transcend time, offering valuable lessons for modern leaders and policymakers. By prioritising the welfare of the people, adhering to ethics, and maintaining strategic foresight, Chanakya's model provides a blueprint for effective and enduring governance.

Managing Resources Wisely: Lessons for Organisations

Chapter 13

Chanakya, the master strategist, emphasised the importance of resource management in the sustainability and growth of any kingdom or organisation. His teachings in the *Arthashastra* provide a remarkably applicable framework to modern organisations striving to use their human, financial, or material resources efficiently.

---

1. Resource Allocation with Purpose

Chanakya believed that every resource should serve a clearly defined purpose. He stated:

"Expenditure must always match income, and resources should be directed towards achieving the state's highest priorities."

For organisations, this means:

- Prioritising investments that align with strategic goals.
- Avoid wasteful spending on non-essential activities.
- Ensuring resources are deployed where they yield the most significant impact.

---

2. The Importance of Planning and Forecasting

Effective management begins with foresight. Chanakya advised leaders to anticipate future needs and challenges. He wrote:

"A king must prepare for times of both abundance and scarcity."

Organisational lessons include:

- Conducting regular financial planning and risk assessments.
- Preparing contingency plans for economic downturns or unexpected challenges.

- Building reserves for long-term sustainability.

---

3. Human Resource Management

Chanakya placed great emphasis on the proper utilisation of human resources. He advocated selecting capable and ethical individuals for key roles, stating:

"The strength of a kingdom lies in the quality of its advisors and administrators."

For modern organisations:

- Invest in recruiting and training skilled employees.
- Ensure alignment between employees' roles and their strengths.
- Promote a culture of accountability, trust, and collaboration.

---

4. Financial Prudence

Chanakya was a staunch advocate of fiscal responsibility. He advised:

"Wealth accumulated unethically will eventually bring ruin."

Organisational practices inspired by this principle include:

- Adhering to ethical financial practices.
- Maintaining transparent accounting and auditing systems.
- Balancing short-term profitability with long-term financial health.

---

5. Asset Optimisation

Chanakya emphasised the efficient use of resources to maximise their value. He stated:

"Unused wealth is as good as wasted wealth."

Lessons for organisations:

- Regularly evaluate the utilisation of assets, such as infrastructure and technology.
- Implement cost-effective solutions to improve operational efficiency.
- Avoid hoarding resources that do not contribute to productivity or profitability.

---

6. Crisis Management and Flexibility

Chanakya's teachings highlight the importance of adaptability during crises. He noted:

"A wise king must be prepared to adapt his strategies to changing circumstances."

For modern businesses:

- Cultivate agility to pivot strategies when faced with challenges.
- Manage resources dynamically during economic or market crises.
- Encourage innovation and resilience within teams.

---

7. Sustainability and Long-Term Thinking

Chanakya believed in ensuring the longevity of resources. He advised:

"Protect and nurture the sources of your wealth; they are the roots of your prosperity."

This translates into:

- Adopting sustainable practices to preserve resources for future generations.
- Investing in renewable energy, eco-friendly technologies, and responsible sourcing.
- Promoting a corporate culture that values environmental and social responsibility.

---

8. Monitoring and Evaluation

Chanakya stressed the need for regular assessment of resource use. He wrote:

"What is not measured cannot be controlled."

In practice, organisations can:

- Set measurable performance metrics for all resource-intensive activities.
- Conduct regular audits to track progress and identify inefficiencies.

- Use data-driven decision-making to refine resource allocation strategies.

---

9. Collaboration and Alliances

Chanakya's diplomatic acumen extended to resource-sharing through alliances. He stated:

"Form alliances that strengthen your position and bring mutual benefits." For organisations:

- Partner with other businesses to share knowledge, infrastructure, or talent.
- Foster collaborative ecosystems within industries for mutual growth.
- Leverage partnerships to access additional resources cost-effectively.

---

10. Rewarding Resourcefulness

Chanakya valued innovation and resourcefulness in his administrators. He encouraged:

"Recognise and reward those who create value from limited resources."

Organisations can:

- Cultivate a culture of innovation to optimise resource use.
- Incentivise employees who propose cost-saving or productivity-enhancing ideas.
- Celebrate achievements that reflect ingenuity and efficiency.

Summary

Chanakya's principles of resource management provide a comprehensive guide for modern organisations. Businesses can achieve greater efficiency and long-term success by prioritising ethical practices, strategic planning, and sustainability. His teachings remind us that wise resource management is not merely about conserving wealth but creating value for all stakeholders.

Building and Sustaining a Team: Trust and Accountability

Chapter 14

One of the most significant aspects of Chanakya's teachings is his emphasis on the strength of a cohesive and reliable team. His principles highlight that no leader can achieve greatness without the support of a well-functioning team bound by trust and accountability. Drawing from his insights, here's how organisations can build and sustain such teams:

---

1. The Foundation of Trust

Chanakya believed trust is the cornerstone of all successful relationships, whether between rulers and advisors or within a team. He stated:
"A leader who inspires trust among his people lays the foundation for unity and progress."

In the modern organisational context:

- Foster open communication to build mutual understanding.
- Demonstrate consistency between words and actions.
- Address conflicts transparently to strengthen relationships.

---

2. Selecting the Right People

Chanakya emphasised recruiting individuals who exhibit both competence and integrity. He advised:

"Place the right person in the right position for the kingdom's prosperity."

Organisations can apply this by:

- Conducting thorough evaluations during hiring.
- Matching roles to individuals' strengths and skills.
- Prioritising ethical conduct alongside professional ability.

---

3. Defining Roles and Responsibilities

Chanakya's governance model relied on clear demarcation of duties. He warned:

"Confusion in responsibilities leads to chaos in the administration."

For modern teams:

- Clearly outline roles and expectations for every team member.
- Avoid overlapping responsibilities to ensure accountability.
- Provide clear guidelines to measure performance.

---

4. Accountability as a Pillar of Success

Accountability ensures that individuals take ownership of their actions. Chanakya believed:

"A leader must hold his ministers accountable, for unchecked power breeds corruption."

Organisations can instil accountability by:

- Establishing clear metrics for success.
- Regularly reviewing team performance.
- Encouraging self-assessment and constructive feedback.

---

5. Encouraging Team Cohesion

Chanakya valued unity among his advisors and warned against internal discord.

He stated:

"Divide within the palace invites ruin; unity ensures strength."

To build cohesion:

- Promote a culture of collaboration over competition.
- Organise team-building activities to foster camaraderie.
- Recognise and celebrate collective achievements.

---

6. Empowering Team Members

Chanakya believed in empowering individuals to perform at their best. He wrote:

"The wise ruler delegates responsibility and trusts capable hands."

Empowerment in organisations involves:

- Delegating authority along with responsibility.
- Encouraging initiative and innovation.
- Providing resources and support for independent decision-making.

---

7. Managing Conflicts Effectively

Conflict resolution was central to Chanakya's governance principles. He advised:

"Resolve disputes quickly to prevent divisions from deepening."

In the workplace:

- Address conflicts promptly and impartially.
- Focus on the issue, not individuals, to avoid personal bias.
- Foster a problem-solving mindset within the team.

---

8. Continuous Development and Feedback

Chanakya's teachings underline the importance of learning and improvement.

He noted:

"A leader grows stronger by learning from his team's feedback and mistakes."

Organisations can adopt this by:

- Providing regular training and upskilling opportunities.
- Encouraging open dialogue for feedback.
- Supporting personal and professional growth of team members.

---

9. Leading by Example

Chanakya believed a leader's actions set the tone for the entire team. He stated:

"A king's character is reflected in his kingdom."

For leaders:

- Model the behaviour you expect from your team.
- Demonstrate commitment, fairness, and resilience.
- Show humility and acknowledge mistakes to inspire trust.

---

10. Rewarding Trust and Accountability

Recognising and rewarding good behaviour reinforces desired outcomes.

Chanakya wrote:

"Reward loyalty and diligence to ensure their continuance."

Organisations can:

- Recognise individual and team achievements publicly.
- Offer incentives for accountability and exceptional performance.
- Create growth opportunities for trustworthy team members.

Summary

Chanakya's principles of trust and accountability are timeless tools for building and sustaining effective teams. By fostering a culture of transparency, integrity, and collaboration, leaders can ensure that their teams achieve success that aligns with the organisation's values. Chanakya's teachings remind us that a unified and accountable team is the backbone of any lasting achievement.

Crisis Management: Strategies for Navigating Challenges

Chapter 15

Chanakya's teachings in the *Arthashastra* are a treasure trove of insights on navigating crises. His emphasis on preparation, adaptability, and decisive action makes his strategies remarkably relevant for modern organisations and leaders. Let's explore his approach to crisis management and how it can guide us in overcoming challenges effectively.

---

1. Anticipate and Prepare for Crises

Chanakya believed that crises are inevitable and that preparation is key to survival. He advised:

"A wise leader foresees difficulties and prepares accordingly."

Modern Application:

- Conduct regular risk assessments to identify potential vulnerabilities.
- Develop contingency plans for economic, operational, or reputational risks.
- Build reserves (financial, human, or material) to weather unexpected challenges.

---

2. Maintain Composure During Crises

Chanakya emphasised the importance of calmness and clarity in difficult situations. He stated:

"Panic weakens the leader, while composure inspires confidence."

Modern Application:

- Train leaders to manage stress and stay level-headed under pressure.
- Focus on solutions rather than dwelling on the problem.
- Encourage teams to maintain a positive and proactive attitude.

---

3. Quick and Decisive Action

Delays in addressing a crisis can exacerbate the situation. Chanakya advised swift action, stating:

"Inaction during a crisis is more dangerous than the crisis itself."

Modern Application:

- Establish protocols for rapid decision-making during emergencies.
- Delegate authority to trusted team members for faster responses.
- Act decisively to mitigate damage and restore normalcy.

---

4. Adaptability and Flexibility

Chanakya's strategies often involved adapting to the changing dynamics of a situation. He noted:

"Adapt your strategies to fit the circumstances; rigidity leads to failure."

Modern Application:

- Foster a culture of agility and innovation within organisations.
- Reevaluate strategies and pivot as necessary during crises.
- Encourage creative problem-solving to overcome unexpected challenges.

---

5. Communication is Key

In times of crisis, clear and transparent communication is essential. Chanakya emphasised:

"A leader must keep his people informed to maintain trust and unity."

Modern Application:

- Provide regular updates to stakeholders, employees, and customers.
- Be honest about challenges while highlighting efforts to resolve them.
- Use multiple communication channels to reach all affected parties effectively.

---

6. Leverage Expertise and Resources

Chanakya valued the counsel of experts and the efficient use of resources during crises. He wrote:

"Consult those with knowledge and experience to find the best path forward."

Modern Application:

- Form crisis management teams with diverse expertise.
- Seek advice from industry experts or external consultants when needed.
- Allocate resources strategically to address the most critical areas.

---

7. Learn from Past Mistakes

Chanakya believed in using past experiences to avoid future pitfalls. He stated:

"Failure is a teacher; learn from it to avoid repeating mistakes."

Modern Application:

- Conduct post-crisis analyses to identify lessons learned.
- Update policies and procedures to prevent similar issues in the future.
- Encourage a growth mindset where failures are seen as opportunities to improve.

---

8. Build Resilience in Advance

Chanakya's philosophy stressed the importance of strength and resilience. He wrote:

"Prepare your defences in times of peace to withstand the storms of war."

Modern Application:

- Invest in employee training and development to enhance capabilities.
- Strengthen organisational structures to withstand disruptions.
- Cultivate a resilient corporate culture that embraces challenges.

---

9. Foster Unity and Collaboration

Chanakya highlighted the power of unity in overcoming adversities. He advised:

"In times of crisis, unity among your people is your greatest strength."

Modern Application:

- Encourage teamwork and collaboration across departments.
- Foster solidarity among employees by emphasising shared goals.
- Leverage partnerships and alliances to pool resources and expertise.

---

10. Keep a Long-Term Perspective

While addressing immediate challenges, Chanakya advised leaders to consider long-term consequences. He stated:

"Act not only for today but also for future generations."

Modern Application:

- Balance short-term fixes with sustainable long-term strategies.
- Use crises as opportunities to innovate and grow.
- Maintain focus on the organisation's mission and vision despite setbacks.

Summary

Chanakya's principles of crisis management emphasise preparation, adaptability, and resilience. His teachings remind us that challenges are obstacles and opportunities to grow stronger and wiser. By applying his strategies, modern leaders can navigate crises effectively, ensuring stability and progress for their organisations.

Financial Wisdom

Part 4

Chanakya's Teachings on Wealth and Economy

Chapter 16

Chanakya, the astute strategist and economist of ancient India, laid down timeless principles on wealth and economy in his treatise, the *Arthashastra.* His teachings emphasise the importance of wealth creation, its ethical utilisation, and the role of a strong economy in ensuring a state's prosperity. These principles remain relevant for individuals, organisations, and nations in modern times.

---

1. Wealth as the Foundation of Stability

Chanakya firmly believed wealth is the backbone of a stable and prosperous society. He wrote:

"Wealth will come from the earth; prosperity depends on economic resources."

Key Insights:

- A strong economy ensures the stability and security of a nation.
- Individuals and organisations should focus on creating sustainable income sources.
- Investment in productive sectors like agriculture, trade, and industry fosters long-term growth.

---

2. The Ethical Pursuit of Wealth

Chanakya emphasised the ethical acquisition and use of wealth. He stated:

"Wealth earned through unethical means destroys the individual and society."

Modern Application:

- Organisations must prioritise ethical practices over short-term profits.

- Leaders should ensure fair wages, transparent dealings, and responsible investments.
- Governments must enforce regulations to prevent exploitation and corruption.

---

3. Savings and Financial Security

Chanakya's teachings stress the importance of saving for unforeseen circumstances. He noted:

"A man must save for the future just as he saves food for the winter."

Practical Lessons:

- Build financial reserves to weather economic downturns or emergencies.
- Encourage personal financial planning and investment in secure assets.
- Nations should maintain fiscal discipline and avoid excessive debt.

---

4. Diversification of Wealth

Chanakya advocated for diversifying income streams to minimise risks. He wrote:

"Do not depend on a single source of income; diversify to ensure stability."

Relevance Today:

- Individuals should explore multiple income sources, such as investments and side businesses.
- Organisations should expand into varied markets and industries.
- Countries must develop diverse economic sectors to reduce reliance on a single industry.

---

5. The Role of Taxation

Chanakya's insights on taxation are both pragmatic and fair. He stated:

"A king should collect taxes like a bee collects honey, without harming the flower."

Modern Implications:

- Governments should design equitable tax systems that encourage

compliance.
- Tax revenues must be utilised for the welfare of citizens and infrastructure development.
- Avoidance of over-taxation ensures economic growth and stability.

---

6. Wealth as a Means, Not an End

Chanakya warned against the obsession with wealth, emphasising its role as a tool for achieving higher goals. He advised:

"Wealth is to be used for the welfare of all, not for selfish indulgence."

Lessons for Leaders:

- Use profits to benefit stakeholders and society at large.
- Prioritise long-term development over short-term material gains.
- Encourage philanthropy and social responsibility.

---

7. Trade and Commerce as Economic Pillars

Chanakya recognised the importance of trade in boosting a nation's economy. He wrote:

"A prosperous state depends on thriving trade and commerce."

Applications:

- Invest in infrastructure such as roads, ports, and technology to facilitate trade.
- Promote free trade agreements and partnerships to expand market reach.
- Support entrepreneurs and businesses to drive economic growth.

---

8. The Role of Governance in Economic Growth

Chanakya viewed good governance as essential for economic prosperity. He stated:

"A well-governed state attracts wealth and investment."

Key Takeaways:

- Leaders should maintain law and order to foster a conducive business environment.

- Transparent policies and ease of doing business attract investments.
- Governments must address economic inequalities to ensure inclusive growth.

---

9. Strategic Use of Resources

Chanakya's approach to resource management focused on efficiency and sustainability. He advised:

"Use resources wisely, for their misuse leads to ruin."

Modern Practices:

- Optimise resource allocation to avoid wastage.
- Invest in renewable energy and sustainable practices.
- Encourage innovation to maximise the utility of limited resources.

---

10. The Interdependence of Wealth and Knowledge

Chanakya emphasised the link between wealth and intellectual growth. He noted:

"Knowledge brings wealth, and wealth sustains knowledge."

Applications:

- Invest in education and research to drive economic development.
- Encourage knowledge-based industries, such as technology and services.
- Align wealth creation with intellectual and cultural advancements.

Summary

Chanakya's teachings on wealth and economy serve as a guiding light for individuals, organisations, and nations striving for prosperity. We can achieve sustainable growth and stability by adhering to his principles of ethical wealth creation, prudent resource management, and fostering economic inclusivity. As Chanakya reminds us, wealth is not merely an end but a means to uplift society and ensure collective well-being.

Financial Planning and Saving: Ancient Insights for Modern Times

Chapter 17

Chanakya, often regarded as the pioneer of economic and strategic thought in ancient India, emphasised the importance of financial planning and saving as foundational pillars of a prosperous life. His teachings in the *Arthashastra* provide timeless wisdom that is remarkably applicable to modern economic management. This chapter explores Chanakya's perspectives on financial prudence and how they can guide individuals and organisations today.

---

1. The Importance of Saving

Chanakya considered saving an essential discipline for financial stability. He noted:

"Just as a bird collects twigs for its nest, a wise person accumulates wealth for future needs."

Key Takeaways:

- Save consistently to build a financial cushion for emergencies.
- Avoid unnecessary expenditures that can erode wealth over time.
- Recognise that disciplined saving is the first step toward achieving financial independence.

Modern Application:

- Create a monthly budget to track income and expenses.
- Automate savings to ensure regular contributions to your financial goals.
- Build an emergency fund covering 6-12 months of essential expenses.

---

2. Planning for the Future

Chanakya's teachings stress the importance of foresight and preparation. He wrote:

"A wise man plans today for the needs of tomorrow."

Practical Lessons:

- Set clear financial goals, both short-term and long-term.
- Invest in assets that offer steady growth and security.
- Prepare for life stages like education, marriage, and retirement.

Modern Application:

- Use financial tools like SIPs (Systematic Investment Plans) and mutual funds for long-term growth.
- Consider life and health insurance as safeguards for unforeseen events.
- Leverage technology to monitor and adjust financial plans regularly.

---

3. Avoiding Debt

Chanakya cautioned against the perils of excessive borrowing. He stated:

"Debt is like a disease; it weakens and consumes the borrower."

Key Insights:

- Borrow only for productive purposes, such as investments or education.
- Avoid lifestyle debt that arises from unnecessary consumption.
- Prioritise repaying loans to avoid long-term financial burdens.

Modern Application:

- Use credit cards judiciously, paying off balances in full each month.
- Avoid high-interest loans unless necessary.
- Establish a debt repayment plan to regain financial stability.

---

4. Diversification of Income and Investments

Chanakya advocated for diversifying income sources and investments to minimise risks. He observed:

"Do not rely on a single source of income; multiple streams ensure stability."

Relevance Today:

- Explore side hustles or freelancing to supplement primary income.

- Diversify investments across equities, bonds, real estate, and gold.
- Avoid putting all savings into a single asset class or venture.

Modern Tools:

- Mutual funds and ETFs (Exchange-Traded Funds) for portfolio diversification.
- Passive income avenues like rental properties or dividend-yielding stocks.
- Professional financial advisors to align investments with goals.

---

5. The Role of Frugality

Chanakya believed in living within one's means and avoiding wastefulness. He stated:

"Wealth saved is wealth earned."

Practical Lessons:

- Differentiate between needs and wants to avoid impulsive spending.
- Adopt a minimalist lifestyle that prioritises quality over quantity.
- Channel saved funds into productive investments.

Modern Practices:

- Use budgeting apps to monitor spending habits.
- Opt for value-based purchasing rather than luxury-driven choices.
- Regularly review and cut unnecessary subscriptions or expenses.

---

6. Investing in Knowledge

Chanakya emphasised the connection between knowledge and wealth. He noted:

"The greatest investment is in education, for it yields the highest returns."

Key Takeaways:

- Invest in skills that enhance earning potential and career growth.
- Stay updated on financial literacy to make informed decisions.
- Encourage a culture of continuous learning to adapt to economic changes.

Modern Tools:

- Enrol in online courses on financial planning and investments.
- Attend seminars and workshops to expand knowledge.
- Leverage books, podcasts, and expert advice to deepen understanding.

---

7. Generosity and Wealth Distribution

Chanakya believed in using wealth for the greater good, stating:

"Wealth unused or hoarded is wasted; share it for the welfare of society."

Modern Implications:

- Allocate a portion of earnings to charitable causes or community support.
- Create scholarships or funds to uplift underprivileged sections of society.
- Ensure that financial success translates into meaningful societal contributions.

Summary

Chanakya's financial planning and saving teachings provide a timeless blueprint for managing wealth effectively. His principles resonate with the modern ethos of economic security and sustainability by emphasising discipline, foresight, and ethical practices. Whether for an individual, a business, or a nation, the art of financial prudence, as outlined by Chanakya, remains a cornerstone of enduring prosperity.

The Art of Investment: Risk and Reward

Chapter 18

Chanakya, the ancient Indian scholar and economist, recognised the complexities of investment and the delicate balance between risk and reward. His principles, articulated in the *Arthashastra*, offer profound insights into making sound financial decisions. In today's volatile markets and economic uncertainties, Chanakya's teachings serve as a timeless guide for individuals, businesses, and governments navigating the intricate landscape of investments.

---

1. The Foundation of Investment: Knowledge and Analysis

Chanakya emphasised the importance of understanding before acting. He stated:

"One who acts without proper knowledge is like a blind man walking on an uneven path."

Key Takeaways:

- Conduct thorough research and analysis before committing resources.
- Understand market trends, risks, and potential returns.
- Avoid impulsive decisions driven by speculation or hearsay.

Modern Application:

- Study financial markets and economic indicators.
- Leverage tools like fundamental and technical analysis for stock investments.
- Consult financial advisors or use educational resources to build investment knowledge.

---

2. Diversification: Spreading Risk

Chanakya's teachings highlight the wisdom of not putting all resources in one place. He advised:

"Do not place all your hopes on a single strategy; always have alternatives."

Practical Lessons:

- Diversify investments across asset classes to mitigate risks.
- Allocate resources to stocks, bonds, real estate, and other instruments.
- Avoid overexposure to a single industry or market.

Modern Tools:

- Use balanced mutual funds or ETFs for diversification.
- Maintain a portfolio that aligns with risk tolerance and financial goals.
- Periodically review and rebalance investments.

---

3. Calculated Risk: The Essence of Reward

Chanakya acknowledged that risk is inherent in any investment but stressed that it must be measured. He wrote:

"Take risks, but only after assessing their consequences."

Relevance Today:

- Recognise the difference between calculated and reckless risk.
- Use risk assessment frameworks like SWOT (Strengths, Weaknesses, Opportunities, Threats).
- Understand the relationship between risk and reward; higher risks often accompany higher potential returns.

Modern Application:

- Use tools like the Sharpe Ratio to evaluate risk-adjusted returns.
- Diversify high-risk investments with safer options.
- Avoid speculative ventures that lack transparency.

---

4. Long-Term Vision: Patience Pays

Chanakya's philosophy underlined the importance of patience in achieving substantial gains. He noted:

"Wealth grows steadily, like a tree watered daily."

Key Insights:

- Investments require time to mature; avoid the trap of instant gratification.

- Focus on long-term growth rather than short-term profits.
- Compound interest and reinvestment yield exponential benefits over time.

Modern Tools:

- Use SIPs (Systematic Investment Plans) to build wealth consistently.
- Invest in retirement funds or index funds for long-term security.
- Stay committed to financial goals despite market fluctuations.

---

5. Avoiding Greed and Fear

Chanakya warned against emotional extremes such as cloud judgment. He advised:

"Control your desires, for unchecked greed leads to downfall."

Practical Lessons:

- Do not chase investments based solely on high returns; evaluate their sustainability.
- Avoid panic-selling during market downturns; focus on the bigger picture.
- Maintain a disciplined approach to investing regardless of market conditions.

Modern Practices:

- Use tools like stop-loss orders to minimise emotional decision-making.
- Follow a structured investment plan rather than reacting to market news.
- Seek professional advice during periods of uncertainty.

---

6. Ethical Investments: Wealth with Responsibility

Chanakya believed that wealth should be used for the greater good. He wrote:

"Wealth earned without harming others brings true happiness."

Modern Implications:

- Invest in socially responsible funds prioritising environmental, social, and governance (ESG) factors.

- Avoid ventures that exploit resources or harm communities.
- Encourage ethical practices in business operations and investments.

---

7. Continuous Monitoring and Adaptation

Chanakya emphasised the need to stay vigilant and adaptable in changing circumstances. He stated:

"The wise adjust their course with changing winds."

Practical Lessons:

- Regularly monitor the performance of your investments.
- Stay updated on economic and geopolitical developments that affect markets.
- Be willing to adapt strategies in response to new opportunities or threats.

Modern Tools:

- Use financial apps and dashboards for real-time tracking.
- Subscribe to market analysis reports for informed decision-making.
- Schedule periodic reviews with financial advisors.

Summary

As Chanakya outlined, the art of investment lies in balancing risk and reward with prudence and foresight. By embracing his principles of knowledge, diversification, ethical practices, and long-term vision, individuals and organisations can navigate the complexities of modern financial systems. Chanakya's teachings remind us that true wealth is not just about accumulation but about creating stability, growth, and shared prosperity.

Balancing Material Wealth with Spiritual Growth

Chapter 19

Chanakya's teachings often combine the pursuit of material wealth with spiritual wisdom, illustrating how seemingly divergent paths can complement each other. For Chanakya, material wealth was a means to achieve societal stability and personal fulfilment, while spiritual growth offered a higher purpose and inner peace. In today's fast-paced world, his insights provide valuable guidance on maintaining this delicate balance.

---

1. Wealth as a Tool, Not an End

Chanakya viewed wealth as a resource to fulfil responsibilities and serve a higher purpose. He stated:

"Wealth, if used properly, brings happiness; if misused, it leads to ruin."

Key Takeaways:

- Material wealth should be a foundation for a fulfilling life, not a sole pursuit.
- Wealth must be used responsibly to support family, community, and personal growth.
- Balance consumption with contributions to society and spiritual endeavours.

Modern Application:

- Allocate a portion of income for philanthropic activities.
- Use wealth to invest in experiences and education that enrich life.
- Avoid materialism by focusing on meaningful achievements.

---

2. Aligning Actions with Dharma

Chanakya emphasised living a life guided by dharma (righteousness). He taught:

"A person who earns wealth while adhering to dharma enjoys true happiness."

Practical Lessons:

- Pursue wealth through ethical means that align with moral values.
- Recognise that spiritual fulfilment comes from living a virtuous life.
- Integrate honesty and integrity into all financial and personal dealings.

Modern Practices:

- Choose careers and businesses that uphold ethical practices.
- Incorporate mindfulness and gratitude into daily routines.
- Practice fairness and transparency in financial transactions.

---

3. The Importance of Detachment

While Chanakya acknowledged the necessity of wealth, he warned against becoming overly attached. He observed:
"Possessions are temporary; only virtues endure."

Key Insights:

- Understand that wealth is impermanent and should not define one's identity.
- Cultivate inner peace through self-awareness and spiritual practices.
- Recognise that true happiness lies beyond material possessions.

Modern Tools:

- Practice minimalism to reduce dependency on material goods.
- Engage in meditation or yoga to strengthen inner resilience.
- Focus on building relationships and experiences over accumulating possessions.

---

4. Wealth and Spiritual Growth as Complementary Goals

Chanakya believed that material and spiritual pursuits are not mutually exclusive. He stated:
"A person who balances wealth and wisdom achieves true greatness."

Relevance Today:

- View wealth to facilitate spiritual and intellectual growth.
- Invest in activities that nurture the soul, such as art, music, or community service.

- Understand that spiritual growth enhances decision-making and personal fulfilment.

Modern Practices:

- Dedicate time to self-reflection and continuous learning.
- Use financial stability to explore hobbies and spiritual interests.
- Participate in volunteer programs to connect with a larger purpose.

---

5. Practicing Gratitude and Contentment

Chanakya emphasised the value of appreciating what one has. He advised:
"Contentment is the greatest wealth."

Practical Lessons:

- Regularly reflect on the blessings and opportunities in life.
- Avoid comparing yourself with others to cultivate genuine contentment.
- Balance ambition with gratitude for present achievements.

Modern Application:

- Maintain a gratitude journal to acknowledge daily positives.
- Celebrate small milestones without focusing solely on future goals.
- Shift focus from material accumulation to personal growth and relationships.

---

6. Spiritual Growth Through Service

Chanakya believed that serving others leads to both spiritual and societal enrichment. He wrote:
"The hand that gives is the hand that gathers virtue."

Key Takeaways:

- Use wealth to uplift others, fostering a sense of purpose and fulfilment.
- Engage in acts of kindness that transcend monetary value.
- Recognise the spiritual satisfaction derived from helping those in need.

Modern Practices:

- Support charitable organisations or start community initiatives.
- Volunteer skills and time for social causes.

- Teach financial literacy or life skills to underprivileged communities.

---

7. Pursuing Inner and Outer Wealth

Chanakya encouraged seeking a balance between external success and inner harmony. He stated:
"A person who cultivates worldly and spiritual wealth is sagacious."

Practical Lessons:

- Dedicate time to personal growth, health, and spirituality.
- Strive for professional success while maintaining ethical boundaries.
- Balance ambition with practices that foster inner peace and self-awareness.

Modern Application:

- Schedule time for meditation, reading, or other enriching activities.
- Set boundaries to prevent work from overshadowing personal life.
- Pursue goals that align with both material and spiritual aspirations.

Summary

Chanakya's teachings remind us that pursuing wealth and spiritual growth need not be conflicting paths. By adopting a balanced approach that emphasises ethical living, gratitude, and a focus on a higher purpose, we can achieve a fulfilling and harmonious life. His wisdom encourages us to view material success as a foundation for spiritual enrichment, ensuring a life of meaning and balance in the modern world.

Relationships and Society

Part 5

Chanakya's View on Human Behaviour and Relationships

Chapter 20

Through his seminal works, such as the Arthashastra and Chanakya Neeti, Chanakya offered profound insights into human behaviour and the dynamics of relationships. He emphasised that understanding human tendencies and fostering meaningful relationships are pivotal for personal and societal success. His teachings remain deeply relevant in decoding human psychology and building lasting connections in today's fast-paced world.

1. The Nature of Human Behaviour

"A person should not be too honest. Straight trees are cut first, and honest people are screwed first."

Chanakya's observations of human behaviour reflect his pragmatic approach to life. He acknowledged that human actions are often driven by self-interest and that navigating the complexities of behaviour requires wisdom and adaptability.

Key Insights:

- Understand that self-preservation and self-interest are fundamental human instincts.
- Balance honesty with discretion to protect oneself from exploitation.
- Observe and analyse the motivations behind others' actions to respond effectively.

2. Building Trust in Relationships

"Before you start a friendship, test the person. Once you have tested, then make them your friend."

Chanakya believed trust is the cornerstone of all relationships but must be earned through careful observation and experience.

Applications:

- Take time to understand the character and values of others before committing to deep relationships.
- Build trust through consistent and reliable actions.
- Avoid blind faith, nurture relationships through mutual respect and accountability.

---

3. The Role of Mutual Benefit in Relationships

"There is some self-interest behind every friendship. There is no friendship without self-interests. This is a bitter truth."

Chanakya's realistic view of relationships highlights the inevitability of self-interest in human connections. However, he saw mutual benefit as a healthy foundation for long-lasting bonds.

Key Takeaways:

- Focus on creating win-win scenarios in relationships.
- Recognise and respect the contributions of others while offering value in return.
- Avoid relationships that are one-sided or exploitative.

---

4. Emotional Intelligence and Relationships

"He who lives in our mind is near though he may actually be far away, but he who is not in our heart is far though he may really be nearby."

Chanakya's teachings highlight the importance of emotional bonds in relationships. Emotional intelligence—understanding and managing emotions—is crucial for building deep and meaningful connections.

Applications:

- Practice empathy to understand the emotions and perspectives of others.
- Communicate effectively to strengthen emotional bonds.
- Resolve conflicts with patience and tact rather than aggression.

---

5. Recognizing Toxic Relationships

"Avoid him who talks sweetly before you but tries to ruin you behind your back, for he is like a pitcher of poison with milk on top."

Chanakya warned against maintaining relationships with individuals who harbour malicious intent. Recognising and distancing oneself from such toxic influences is essential for personal well-being.

Tips:

- Observe actions rather than merely trusting words.
- Set boundaries with individuals who exhibit harmful behaviour.
- Surround yourself with people who genuinely support and uplift you.

---

6. The Balance of Attachment and Detachment

"Too much attachment leads to fear and sorrow. Detachment is the key to freedom."

Chanakya advocated a balanced relationship approach, where attachment does not lead to dependency or suffering.

Practical Advice:

- Maintain a healthy balance between emotional closeness and independence.
- Avoid clinging to relationships that no longer serve your growth.
- Cultivate self-reliance to reduce emotional vulnerabilities.

---

7. The Importance of Respect and Equality

"Treat your child like a darling for the first five years. For the next five years, scold them. By the time they turn sixteen, treat them like a friend."

Chanakya believed in nurturing relationships with respect and adaptability. This principle applies not only to parenting but also to friendships, partnerships, and professional connections.

Key Takeaways:

- Respect individuality and adapt your approach based on the evolving nature of relationships.
- Promote equality and mutual understanding in all interactions.
- Value the perspectives and contributions of others to foster meaningful connections.

---

8. Leveraging Relationships for Greater Good

"He who is overly attached to his family members experiences fear and sorrow, for the root

of all grief is attachment. Thus, one should discard attachment to be happy."

Chanakya's teachings emphasise using relationships to achieve personal growth and contribute to societal well-being rather than becoming overly entangled in attachments.

Applications:

- Use your relationships to inspire and support collective progress.
- Strike a balance between personal responsibilities and broader societal contributions.
- Share knowledge and resources to uplift others within your network.

Summary

Chanakya's perspectives on human behaviour and relationships offer timeless lessons for navigating the complexities of interpersonal dynamics. Individuals can build meaningful connections that enrich their lives by fostering trust, mutual benefit, emotional intelligence, and respect. Simultaneously, practising detachment and recognising toxic influences ensures these relationships remain healthy and fulfilling. In a world driven by constant interaction, Chanakya's wisdom is a guiding light for cultivating authentic and harmonious relationships.

Building Networks: The Importance of Mutual Benefit

Chapter 21

Chanakya, known for his exceptional strategies in politics and governance, recognised the value of strong networks and alliances. His teachings emphasise that successful personal or professional relationships are built on mutual benefit. This chapter explores how Chanakya's insights can guide individuals in forming, maintaining, and leveraging networks effectively.

---

1. The Foundation of Networking: Trust and Reciprocity

"Even if the enemy is weak, do not challenge them without a strategy; even if a friend is strong, never stop nurturing the bond."

Chanakya highlighted the importance of trust and strategic collaboration in relationships. Trust is the currency of all meaningful connections, and reciprocity ensures longevity.

Applications:

- Build trust through consistent, honest, and transparent communication.
- Focus on creating value for others before seeking benefits for yourself.
- Strengthen bonds by acknowledging and appreciating the contributions of others.

---

2. Identifying Strategic Alliances

"Before forming alliances, assess the strengths, weaknesses, and motives of all parties involved."

Chanakya's emphasis on due diligence in alliances remains relevant in modern networking.

Key Insights:

- Align with individuals and organisations whose values and goals complement yours.
- Assess the potential benefits and risks of partnerships before committing.
- Diversify your network to include mentors, peers, and collaborators from various fields.

---

3. The Principle of Mutual Benefit

"Help others achieve their goals, and they will help you achieve yours."

Chanakya's approach to relationships was inherently symbiotic. He believed in fostering relationships that benefit both parties.

Applications:

- Offer support, knowledge, or resources that others find valuable.
- Seek win-win solutions in collaborations, ensuring mutual growth.
- Avoid one-sided relationships that drain resources without offering value in return.

---

4. Maintaining and Strengthening Networks

"Relationships, like plants, need regular care and attention to thrive."

Building a network is the first step; maintaining it requires consistent effort.

Tips:

- Stay in touch with your connections through regular updates and meaningful conversations.
- Celebrate their successes and support them during challenges.
- Be proactive in renewing dormant connections by finding common grounds for interaction.

---

5. Leveraging Networks for Personal and Professional Growth

"A single wheel cannot move the cart; a strong cart needs all its wheels working together."
Chanakya's analogy underscores the collective power of networks.

Applications:

- Seek advice and mentorship from experienced individuals in your network.
- Collaborate with peers to enhance skills, share resources, and achieve common goals.
- Use your network to gain insights into opportunities and trends in your field.

---

6. Avoiding Pitfalls in Networking

"Do not be overly dependent on anyone. Self-reliance is your greatest strength."

While networks are valuable, over-reliance can lead to vulnerabilities.

Guidelines:

- Balance external support with self-reliance and individual effort.
- Avoid opportunistic behaviour that could damage your reputation.
- Be selective about the relationships you invest in to ensure alignment with your values and goals.

---

7. Networking in the Digital Age

Chanakya's principles adapt seamlessly to modern networking platforms and technologies.

Strategies:

- Use social media and professional platforms to connect with like-minded individuals and organisations.
- Share valuable content to establish your expertise and attract meaningful connections.
- Engage authentically, avoiding superficial interactions or over-automation.

Summary

Chanakya's wisdom on building and sustaining networks underscores the importance of trust, mutual benefit, and strategic thinking. By fostering relationships rooted in reciprocity and shared goals, individuals can create robust networks that drive personal and professional success. The principle of mutual benefit ensures that these connections remain meaningful and enduring, making them invaluable assets in every sphere of life.

Family and Society: A Harmonious Coexistence

Chapter 22

Chanakya's wisdom extends deeply into familial and societal relationships. His teachings underscore the interdependence of strong family units and a thriving society. By fostering harmony, trust, and mutual respect, Chanakya believed that families could be the foundational building blocks for a prosperous community.

---

1. The Role of Family in Shaping Individuals

"One who is too attached to family members experiences fear and sorrow, for the root of all grief is attachment."

Chanakya's philosophy highlights the dual role of families in providing support and cultivating independence. He acknowledged the importance of families in instilling values and discipline, while cautioning against over-dependence.

Key Insights:

- Families provide emotional, educational, and ethical grounding.
- A balanced attachment fosters individual growth without creating excessive dependencies.
- Parents and elders play a pivotal role in nurturing resilience and responsibility.

---

2. Harmony Within the Family

"A house divided will not stand."

Chanakya emphasised unity and mutual respect as the cornerstones of a harmonious household.

Applications:

- Encourage open communication among family members to resolve conflicts amicably.
- Cultivate shared goals and values that strengthen familial bonds.

- Show gratitude and understanding to maintain emotional balance within the family.

---

4. The Family's Contribution to Society

"As a single stick breaks easily, but a bundle of sticks is unbreakable, unity is strength."

Families are microcosms of society. A strong, value-driven family contributes positively to societal well-being.

Key Takeaways:

- Families instil a sense of community and responsibility in individuals.
- Ethical and disciplined family units promote societal harmony.
- Societal progress begins with fostering kindness, empathy, and integrity at home.

---

5. Balancing Individual and Collective Needs

"Just as the bees collect honey in the hive, a family must balance individual efforts with collective prosperity."

Chanakya believed that while individual growth is essential, it should not come at the expense of family or societal harmony.

Applications:

- Encourage individual pursuits that align with the collective welfare of the family.
- Balance personal ambitions with contributions to family goals.
- Promote shared responsibilities to strengthen bonds and ensure equitable growth.

---

6. Strengthening Societal Relationships

"Society thrives on mutual respect and cooperation."

Chanakya recognised that social harmony is built on trust, accountability, and collaboration among its members.

Key Practices:

- Engage in community-building activities to foster stronger societal connections.
- Contribute time, resources, and skills to community welfare.
- Lead by example, promoting ethical and respectful interactions.

---

7. The Interdependence of Family and Society

Chanakya's teachings illustrate how families and societies influence and sustain each other.

Core Principles:

- A society's values are reflected in the upbringing provided by families.
- Thriving families create stable societies, and strong societies provide supportive environments for families.
- Education, cultural traditions, and ethical practices bridge individual households and the larger community.

Summary

Chanakya's insights on family and society offer a timeless guide for achieving harmonious coexistence. By fostering strong familial ties rooted in mutual respect and shared values, individuals can contribute to a thriving culture. Similarly, society ensures its long-term prosperity and stability by supporting family welfare. Family and society form a symbiotic relationship, each nurturing the other to create a balanced and fulfilled life.

The Role of Trust and Communication

Chapter 23

Trust and communication are the twin pillars of any thriving personal, professional, or societal relationship. Chanakya, the astute thinker and strategist, emphasised the profound impact of these elements in fostering stability and growth. His insights, though ancient, resonate deeply in modern times, especially in contexts such as leadership, organisational dynamics, and governance.

---

1. Trust as the Bedrock of Relationships

Chanakya highlighted the essential role of trust in building enduring bonds.

He stated:

"When there is mutual trust, even the impossible becomes possible."

Key Lessons:

- Trust forms the foundation of cooperation and collaboration.
- Broken trust is difficult to restore; it must be nurtured with care.
- A trustworthy leader inspires loyalty and commitment.

Modern Applications:

- Build credibility by aligning words with actions.
- Foster an open environment where trust can flourish.
- Encourage accountability at all levels of interaction.

---

2. Communication: The Bridge to Understanding

Chanakya believed in the power of clear and effective communication. He wrote:

"Speak only after weighing your words, for they can build or break relationships."

Key Insights:

- Effective communication eliminates misunderstandings and fosters clarity.
- Tone and timing are as important as the content of the message.
- Active listening is a vital aspect of meaningful dialogue.

Practical Strategies:

- Use concise and transparent language in professional settings.
- Practice active listening to understand different perspectives.
- Adapt communication styles to suit the audience or context.

---

3. The Interdependence of Trust and Communication

Chanakya's teachings underscore the interconnectedness of trust and communication. He observed:

"Trust grows with honest words and diminishes with deceit."

Relevance Today:

- Honest and transparent communication strengthens trust.
- Misinformation or lack of communication breeds suspicion.
- Regular interactions build rapport and mutual understanding.

Modern Applications:

- Use feedback loops to maintain trust within teams and organisations.
- Address conflicts promptly with open and respectful dialogue.
- Share information regularly to avoid creating a vacuum of mistrust.

---

4. Building Trust in Leadership

Chanakya's philosophy highlighted the leader's role in establishing trust. He stated:

"A leader's integrity inspires the trust of the people."

Leadership Principles:

- Lead by example to demonstrate commitment and reliability.

- Maintain consistency in decision-making and communication.
- Recognise and address issues that may erode trust.

Practical Lessons:

- Build relationships with stakeholders through transparent policies.
- Encourage open forums for employees to voice concerns.
- Reward trustworthy behaviour to reinforce a culture of integrity.

---

5. Navigating Crisis with Trust and Communication

Chanakya recognised the importance of trust and communication in times of crisis. He advised:

"In adversity, clear communication calms fear, and trust strengthens resolve."

Key Insights:

- In crises, people look for honest leaders who communicate openly.
- Avoid hiding facts, as it can damage credibility and trust.
- Timely updates and reassurance help maintain stability.

Modern Practices:

- Use consistent and transparent messaging during organisational changes.
- Ensure communication channels are accessible to all stakeholders.
- Build a crisis management team that prioritises trust and communication.

---

6. Trust and Communication in Teams

Chanakya valued teamwork and recognised the importance of trust and communication within groups. He wrote:

"A united group, bound by trust, achieves more than individuals working alone."

Lessons for Teams:

- Mutual trust enhances collaboration and productivity.
- Open communication allows for the free flow of ideas.
- Acknowledge contributions to build a culture of respect and trust.

Modern Applications:

- Use collaborative tools to enhance team communication.
- Organise regular team-building activities to strengthen bonds.
- Address conflicts constructively to maintain harmony.

---

7. Sustaining Trust Over Time

Chanakya emphasised that trust, once built, must be preserved with consistent effort. He stated:

"Trust, like a delicate thread, is hard to mend once broken."

Practical Insights:

- Avoid actions that may jeopardise trust, such as dishonesty or negligence.
- Regularly communicate to reaffirm trust and understanding.
- Apologise and take corrective action when trust is breached.

Modern Applications:

- Conduct regular evaluations to ensure alignment with stakeholders' expectations.
- Build long-term relationships through consistent engagement.
- Use empathy and transparency to rebuild trust if it falters.

Summary

Chanakya's wisdom on trust and communication underscores their centrality in fostering meaningful and productive relationships. By integrating his teachings into modern practices, individuals and organisations can build stronger connections, resolve conflicts effectively, and achieve enduring success. In Chanakya's words, trust and communication are not mere tools but the essence of harmonious and prosperous coexistence.

Timeless Lessons for Life

Part 6

The Pursuit of Dharma: Living a Principled Life

Chapter 24

Dharma, a cornerstone of Indian philosophy, is often translated as righteousness or duty, but its true essence extends beyond mere morality. It embodies the principles and values that uphold the harmony of life, guiding individuals to act in ways that benefit themselves and society. Chanakya's teachings place dharma at the heart of a meaningful and prosperous existence, offering timeless insights into how one can align actions with higher ideals.

---

1. Understanding Dharma

Chanakya believed that dharma is the foundation for a balanced life. He stated:

"Dharma sustains those who sustain dharma."

Key Insights:

- Dharma is a dynamic concept that evolves with context but remains rooted in universal values.
- It encompasses duties toward oneself, family, society, and the natural world.
- Adhering to dharma ensures long-term stability and harmony.

Modern Relevance:

- Define personal and professional values that guide decision-making.
- Balance individual aspirations with responsibilities toward others.
- Cultivate an ethical approach to work and relationships.

---

2. Dharma as a Guiding Principle in Leadership

For Chanakya, leaders bear a profound responsibility to uphold dharma. He observed:

"A leader who adheres to dharma earns the trust and respect of the people."

Lessons for Leaders:

- Act with integrity and fairness to inspire confidence.
- Prioritise the greater good over personal gain.
- Use power and resources to serve and uplift others.

Modern Applications:

- Promote ethical practices in organisations and institutions.
- Ensure policies and actions align with societal welfare.
- Lead by example to foster a culture of accountability.

---

3. Balancing Dharma with Artha and Kama

Chanakya's philosophy acknowledges the human pursuit of artha (wealth) and kama (desire) but emphasises that dharma must govern these. He advised:

"Without dharma, wealth and desires lead to ruin."

Key Takeaways:

- Material and emotional pursuits are legitimate but must be aligned with ethical boundaries.
- Dharma ensures that these pursuits contribute to personal growth and societal harmony.

Practical Strategies:

- Establish clear ethical guidelines for financial and personal goals.
- Practice moderation to avoid excesses that disrupt balance.
- Use resources and relationships to support constructive endeavours.

---

4. The Role of Dharma in Crisis Management

In times of adversity, adhering to dharma provides clarity and direction. Chanakya emphasised:

"In moments of doubt, let dharma be your guide."

Crisis Management Lessons:

- Stay committed to principles even under pressure.

- Avoid short-term gains that compromise long-term integrity.
- Use dharma as a compass to navigate uncertainty and conflict.

Modern Practices:

- Develop a crisis response plan rooted in ethical considerations.
- Maintain transparency to build trust during challenging times.
- Encourage dialogue to address diverse perspectives.

---

5. Personal Dharma: The Path to Inner Peace

Chanakya taught that living by one's dharma leads to self-fulfilment and peace. He wrote:

"Contentment comes to those who walk the path of dharma."

Key Insights:

- Recognise and fulfil personal responsibilities to achieve harmony.
- Dharma varies for each individual based on roles and circumstances.
- Aligning actions with dharma fosters inner satisfaction and reduces stress.

Steps for Implementation:

- Reflect regularly on personal values and goals.
- Take responsibility for actions and their consequences.
- Seek a balance between personal needs and societal expectations.

---

6. Dharma in Relationships

Chanakya highlighted the importance of dharma in fostering healthy relationships. He stated:

"Relationships thrive when rooted in respect and duty."

Lessons for Nurturing Bonds:

- Honour commitments and responsibilities toward loved ones.
- Cultivate empathy and understanding to strengthen connections.
- Avoid selfish actions that harm trust and harmony.

Modern Relevance:

- Practice active listening and open communication.
- Support family, friends, and colleagues in their times of need.
- Uphold fairness and mutual respect in all interactions.

---

7. Dharma as a Collective Responsibility

Chanakya's teachings extend dharma to societal and environmental contexts. He asserted:

"The welfare of the many lies in the adherence to dharma by all."

Key Principles:

- Individuals and organisations share a duty to contribute to societal progress.
- Protecting nature and resources is an integral part of dharma.

Practical Applications:

- Support community initiatives that promote education and well-being.
- Adopt sustainable practices to reduce environmental impact.
- Advocate for policies that prioritise equity and justice.

Summary

The pursuit of dharma, as envisioned by Chanakya, is a timeless framework for living a principled and harmonious life. By integrating his teachings into personal and professional practices, individuals can achieve balance, contribute to societal progress, and experience profound fulfilment. Chanakya's wisdom reminds us that the path of dharma is not always easy, but it is invariably rewarding, leading to a life of integrity, peace, and enduring success.

Overcoming Adversity: Chanakya's Guidance on Resilience

Chapter 25

Adversity is an inevitable part of life, testing the strength, resolve, and character of individuals and organisations alike. The legendary strategist and thinker Chanakya offered profound wisdom on navigating challenges with resilience and determination. His teachings illuminate the paths to overcoming obstacles and emerging stronger through perseverance, adaptability, and foresight.

---

1. Resilience as a Virtue

Chanakya regarded resilience as an essential quality for leaders and individuals. He said:

"One who persists through difficulties with patience and determination will ultimately succeed."

Key Insights:

- Resilience is the ability to endure hardships without losing focus on goals.
- Patience and determination are critical components of overcoming adversity.
- Challenges are opportunities for growth and self-improvement.

Practical Applications:

- Developmental fortitude through consistent self-reflection and discipline.
- Stay focused on long-term goals despite short-term setbacks.
- Build a support system to encourage during tough times.

---

2. The Power of Adaptability

Chanakya emphasised the importance of adapting to changing

circumstances. He observed:

"When the wind changes direction, adjust your sails to reach the destination."

Lessons on Adaptability:

- Flexibility enables individuals to respond effectively to unexpected challenges.
- Rigidity in thought or action can lead to failure in dynamic situations.
- Innovation and creativity often emerge from adapting to adversity.

Modern Applications:

- Embrace change as an opportunity to learn and grow.
- Develop contingency plans to prepare for unforeseen events.
- Cultivate an open mind to explore new strategies and solutions.

---

3. Learning from Failure

Chanakya's teachings encourage viewing failure as a stepping stone to success. He stated:

"Failures are but lessons in the larger journey of achievement."

Key Takeaways:

- Failure provides valuable insights into what needs improvement.
- Fear of failure should not deter one from pursuing meaningful goals.
- Resilience grows more potent when one learns to bounce back from setbacks.

Practical Lessons:

- Analyse failures objectively to identify areas for improvement.
- Reframe failures as learning experiences rather than defeats.
- Use past setbacks to build confidence and refine strategies.

---

4. Maintaining Focus and Discipline

Chanakya stressed the need for unwavering focus and discipline during challenging times. He wrote:

"Discipline is the bridge between goals and achievements, especially in adversity."

Key Insights:

- Distractions and negativity can derail progress during crises.
- A disciplined approach ensures consistency and progress.
- Focus sharpens problem-solving abilities and enhances resilience.

Practical Strategies:

- Set clear, achievable objectives to maintain direction.
- Establish daily routines that reinforce discipline and productivity.
- Practice mindfulness to stay centred and reduce stress.

---

5. Foresight and Planning

Chanakya's strategic acumen highlighted the importance of planning for adversity. He advised:

"Prepare for the worst while striving for the best."

Lessons in Foresight:

- Anticipating challenges allows for proactive measures.
- Long-term planning minimises the impact of unexpected crises.
- A well-prepared individual or organisation can weather storms with confidence.

Modern Practices:

- Conduct regular risk assessments to identify potential vulnerabilities.
- Build financial and emotional reserves for emergencies.
- Train teams to respond effectively to unforeseen situations.

---

6. Inner Strength and Emotional Resilience

Chanakya recognised the importance of emotional resilience in overcoming adversity. He remarked:

"Strength comes not just from physical endurance but from mental fortitude."

Key Takeaways:

- Emotional resilience enables individuals to remain calm under pressure.
- A positive mindset fosters hope and determination.
- Developing self-awareness enhances emotional regulation.

Steps to Build Emotional Resilience:

- Practice self-care to maintain mental and physical health.
- Cultivate a positive outlook through gratitude and optimism.
- Seek guidance from mentors or peers during challenging times.

---

7. Collective Strength in Adversity

Chanakya's teachings often emphasised the value of collective effort. He observed:

"Unity is strength, and together, obstacles become surmountable."

Key Lessons:

- Collaboration fosters mutual support and shared problem-solving.
- Trust and communication are essential for team resilience.
- Communities can achieve remarkable outcomes through collective determination.

Practical Applications:

- Encourage teamwork to pool resources and ideas.
- Build strong networks for mutual support during crises.
- Recognise and celebrate collective achievements to boost morale.

Summary

Chanakya's guidance on resilience offers a roadmap for overcoming adversity with grace and determination. By embracing his principles of adaptability, discipline, emotional strength, and collective effort, individuals and organisations can navigate challenges and emerge stronger. His wisdom reminds us that adversity is not a roadblock but a stepping stone to growth and success. As Chanakya taught, the accurate measure of strength lies in the ability to rise after every fall, forging ahead with unwavering resolve.

The Legacy of Chanakya: Lessons for Future Generations

Chapter 26

Chanakya, a beacon of wisdom and strategy, left an indelible mark on Indian history and thought. Known as Kautilya or Vishnugupta, he was not only the architect of the Mauryan Empire but also the author of *Arthashastra*, a treatise on statecraft, economics, and governance. Though rooted in ancient times, his teachings resonate with relevance for future generations, offering profound insights into leadership, ethics, strategy, and personal growth.

---

1. Visionary Leadership

Chanakya's ability to envision a united and powerful India was revolutionary. He demonstrated that strong leadership can transform societies and nations. He believed:

"A leader is one who knows the way, goes the way, and shows the way."

Lessons for Future Leaders:

- Cultivate a clear vision that aligns with long-term goals.
- Lead by example to inspire trust and commitment.
- Adapt leadership styles to the needs of the time while maintaining core values.

---

2. The Art of Strategy

Chanakya's strategic brilliance was instrumental in overthrowing the Nanda dynasty and establishing the Mauryan Empire. His strategies emphasised foresight, adaptability, and meticulous planning.

"Before you start some work, always ask yourself three questions: Why am I doing it? What might the results be? Will I be successful?"

Key Takeaways:

- Strategic thinking requires understanding both opportunities and threats.

- Planning and preparation are critical to achieving objectives.
- Success is often determined by the ability to anticipate challenges and adapt.

---

3. Ethics and Governance

For Chanakya, governance was not merely about power but about responsibility. He underscored the role of ethics in creating a just and stable society.

"The happiness of the people is the ruler's happiness; their welfare is his welfare."

Modern Applications:

- Prioritise ethical practices in leadership and governance.
- Focus on the welfare of stakeholders to ensure sustainable progress.
- Recognise the long-term value of trust and integrity in societal development.

---

4. Education and Knowledge

Chanakya's life exemplified the transformative power of education. He valued knowledge as the ultimate tool for empowerment and progress.

"Education is the best friend. An educated person is respected everywhere. Education beats the beauty and the youth."

Lessons for Future Generations:

- Lifelong learning is essential for personal and professional growth.
- Knowledge must be applied to solve real-world problems.
- Education is the foundation of innovation and societal advancement.

---

5. Economic Wisdom

Chanakya's economic principles in the *Arthashastra* emphasised wealth creation, resource management, and fiscal responsibility.

"Wealth, if not managed properly, can lead to one's downfall."

Key Insights:

- Promote entrepreneurship and innovation to foster economic growth.
- Manage resources wisely to ensure sustainability and equity.
- Balance material pursuits with ethical considerations.

---

6. Resilience and Determination

Chanakya's life was a testament to perseverance. He remained committed to building a strong and unified empire despite facing numerous setbacks.

"A person should not be too honest. Straight trees are cut first, and honest people are screwed first."

Practical Guidance:

- Cultivate resilience to navigate adversity and challenges.
- Be pragmatic in approach while upholding core values.
- Learn from failures and use them as stepping stones to success.

---

7. The Balance Between Dharma, Artha, and Kama

Chanakya's philosophy emphasised the harmony between spiritual and material pursuits. He taught that true fulfilment lies in balancing Dharma (duty), Artha (wealth), and Kama (desires).

"He who is overly attached to his family experiences fear and sorrow, for the root of all grief is attachment."

Key Takeaways:

- Avoid excessive attachment to material possessions.
- Align personal goals with ethical and societal responsibilities.
- Strive for holistic growth that encompasses spiritual, emotional, and material dimensions.

---

8. The Importance of Unity and Collaboration

Chanakya's efforts to unite the Indian subcontinent demonstrated the power of collective effort.

"United we stand, divided we fall."

Lessons for Society:

- Foster teamwork and collaboration to achieve shared goals.
- Build alliances based on trust and mutual respect.
- Recognise diversity as a strength that enriches collective endeavours.

---

9. Timeless Relevance of Chanakya's Teachings

Chanakya's principles transcend time and geography. His insights into governance, strategy, and personal development remain valuable in today's complex world.

Key Messages:

- Chanakya's teachings provide a holistic framework for navigating modern challenges.
- His emphasis on ethics, education, and resilience is especially relevant in a rapidly changing world.
- By integrating his wisdom, future generations can build a more just, prosperous, and harmonious society.

Summary

Chanakya's legacy is a treasure trove of knowledge and wisdom, offering guidance for individuals, leaders, and societies. His teachings continue to inspire and empower, reminding us that true greatness lies in the pursuit of knowledge, the practice of ethics, and the resilience to overcome challenges. By embracing Chanakya's principles, future generations can forge paths of progress and leave lasting impacts on the world.

Summary

The Enduring Relevance of Chanakya in Modern Life

Chapter 27

Chanakya, the ancient Indian philosopher, strategist, and statesman, remains relevant even in the 21st century. Known for his treatises such as *Arthashastra* and *Chanakya Neeti*, he laid down principles of governance, economics, ethics, and personal conduct that resonate deeply in today's fast-changing world. His teachings transcend time, offering timeless wisdom that addresses the complexities of modern life.

---

1. Governance and Leadership

Chanakya's principles of governance emphasise ethical leadership and accountability. His ideas on statecraft, administrative efficiency, and public welfare are as applicable today as they were centuries ago.

"The happiness of the people is the ruler's happiness; their welfare is his welfare."

Relevance Today:

- Governments and corporate leaders alike can adopt Chanakya's focus on prioritising the well-being of their people.
- Ethical governance fosters trust and ensures sustainable development.
- Leadership should embody vision, decisiveness, and moral responsibility.

---

2. Strategic Thinking

Chanakya's strategic brilliance was instrumental in uniting a fragmented India and establishing the Mauryan Empire. His emphasis on foresight, preparation, and adaptability provides a roadmap for modern decision-making.

"Before you start some work, always ask yourself three questions: Why am I doing it? What might the results be? Will I be successful?"

Relevance Today:

- Strategic planning is crucial for individuals and organisations to navigate uncertainties.
- Foresight and preparation help in mitigating risks and capitalising on opportunities.
- Adaptability to changing circumstances is vital in an interconnected global economy.

---

3. Economics and Financial Management

Chanakya's insights into economics emphasised wealth creation, resource allocation, and fiscal discipline. His teachings underscore the importance of balancing economic growth with ethical practices.

"Wealth, if not managed properly, can lead to one's downfall."

Relevance Today:

- Modern economies can benefit from his principles of efficient resource management and prudent financial planning.
- Individuals can learn to balance spending and saving, ensuring financial stability.
- Ethical business practices are essential for long-term success.

---

4. Ethics and Morality

Chanakya emphasised ethical conduct and moral responsibility in both personal and professional life. He believed that a foundation of integrity is essential for sustainable success.

"A person should not be too honest. Straight trees are cut first, and honest people are screwed first."

Relevance Today:

- While the world evolves, the importance of maintaining integrity remains constant.
- Ethical dilemmas in business, governance, and personal life can be navigated by adhering to core moral principles.
- Long-term trust and credibility are built on ethical foundations.

---

5. Education and Continuous Learning

Chanakya's life demonstrates the transformative power of education. He championed knowledge as the ultimate wealth that empowers individuals and societies.

"Education is the best friend. An educated person is respected everywhere. Education beats the beauty and the youth."

Relevance Today:

- In an era of rapid technological advancement, continuous learning is essential for staying relevant.
- Education fosters innovation, critical thinking, and informed decision-making.
- Societal progress hinges on accessible and equitable education.

---

6. Resilience and Perseverance

Challenges and setbacks marked Chanakya's life, but his resilience enabled him to succeed remarkably. He advocated for determination and perseverance in overcoming adversity.

"Even if a snake is not poisonous, it should pretend to be venomous."

Relevance Today:

- Resilience is a critical skill for navigating the uncertainties of modern life.
- Perseverance helps individuals and organisations achieve long-term goals despite obstacles.
- Building mental strength and adaptability ensures success in an ever-changing environment.

---

7. Balancing Material and Spiritual Pursuits

Chanakya's philosophy advocated for a balanced approach to life, integrating material success with spiritual growth and ethical living.

"He who is overly attached to his family members experiences fear and sorrow, for the root of all grief is attachment."

Relevance Today:

- In a world driven by material pursuits, his teachings remind us of the importance of mindfulness and balance.
- Prioritising mental and emotional well-being alongside professional success leads to a fulfilling life.
- Spiritual growth fosters inner peace and ethical decision-making.

Summary

Chanakya's teachings offer a comprehensive guide for navigating modern challenges. His principles, from governance and leadership to personal development and financial management, provide a framework for building a successful and balanced life. As the world becomes increasingly complex and interconnected, Chanakya's wisdom is a timeless beacon, inspiring individuals and societies to strive for ethical excellence, strategic brilliance, and holistic growth.

Applying Chanakya's Teachings in Everyday Situations

Chapter 28

Though rooted in ancient times, Chanakya's teachings offer pragmatic solutions for daily challenges. His insights into human behaviour, leadership, ethics, and strategy provide a blueprint for effectively navigating modern life. This chapter explores how Chanakya's wisdom can be applied to common situations, empowering individuals to lead more balanced and purposeful lives.

---

1. Time Management: Prioritising the Essentials

"A man is great by deeds, not by birth."

Chanakya's philosophy emphasises the importance of purposeful action. In today's fast-paced world, managing time effectively is essential.

Application:

- Prioritise tasks based on their impact and urgency.
- Avoid procrastination by setting clear, achievable goals.
- Dedicate time to self-improvement and learning, as Chanakya considered knowledge the foundation of success.

---

2. Handling Relationships with Wisdom

"Never share your secrets with anybody. It will destroy you."

Chanakya's caution about discretion underscores the need for trust and boundaries in relationships.

Application:

- Foster trust with honesty but maintain boundaries to protect personal and professional integrity.
- Address conflicts with empathy and logic, avoiding emotional impulsiveness.

- Build networks strategically by forming meaningful connections.

---

3. Financial Discipline

"Before you start some work, always ask yourself three questions: Why am I doing it? What might the results be? Will I be successful?"

Chanakya's focus on planning and foresight extends to financial management, urging individuals to live within their means.

Application:

- Create a budget and track expenses to ensure financial stability.
- Invest in long-term assets rather than succumbing to impulsive spending.
- Build an emergency fund as a buffer against unforeseen challenges.

---

4. Decision-Making in Complex Situations

"A person should not be too honest. Straight trees are cut first, and honest people are screwed first."

While advocating for ethics, Chanakya also recognised the need for practicality in decision-making.

Application:

- Balance honesty with tact to navigate challenging situations.
- Evaluate decisions logically, considering both short-term and long-term consequences.
- Remain flexible and adapt strategies as circumstances evolve.

---

5. Self-Discipline and Personal Growth

"Education is the best friend. An educated person is respected everywhere. Education beats the beauty and the youth."

Chanakya's emphasis on self-discipline and education as tools for empowerment remains profoundly relevant.

Application:

- Cultivate daily habits that promote discipline, such as regular exercise, reading, or meditation.

- Pursue continuous learning to enhance skills and broaden perspectives.
- Set personal benchmarks to measure progress and stay motivated.

---

6. Overcoming Adversity with Resilience

"Even if a snake is not poisonous, it should pretend to be venomous."

Chanakya advocated for resilience and strategic thinking to overcome challenges.

Application:

- Face adversities with a calm and composed mindset.
- Develop contingency plans to handle unexpected situations.
- Use setbacks as opportunities for growth and learning.

---

7. Ethical Leadership at Home and Work

"The king who is devoted to dharma, virtuous in conduct, and who keeps his subjects happy, will enjoy sovereignty for a long time."

Leadership, according to Chanakya, is rooted in ethics and service.

Application:

- Lead by example, inspiring trust and loyalty in personal and professional life.
- Make decisions that balance personal gains with collective well-being.
- Encourage open communication and create an environment of mutual respect.

---

8. Strategic Thinking in Everyday Life

"As soon as the fear approaches near, attack and destroy it."

Chanakya's approach to strategy emphasises preparedness and decisive action.

Application:

- Anticipate potential challenges and address them proactively.
- Set clear objectives and devise plans to achieve them efficiently.
- Stay vigilant and adaptable to changing circumstances.

Summary

Chanakya's wisdom provides actionable insights for navigating daily life with purpose and confidence. His teachings offer a timeless guide, whether managing time, building relationships, handling finances, or making decisions. By integrating these principles into everyday situations, individuals can cultivate resilience, achieve personal and professional success, and lead a life of balance and integrity.

Appendices

Multiple Choice Questions (MCQs) on Chanakya Niti

Section 1: General Principles of Chanakya Niti

1. What does Chanakya emphasise as the most critical trait for a king?

    a) Wealth
    b) Intelligence
    c) Justice
    d) Courage

2. According to Chanakya, what is the root cause of all evil?

    a) Ignorance
    b) Greed
    c) Anger
    d) Fear

3. Chanakya advises avoiding which type of person as a friend.

    a) Wise
    b) Brave
    c) Hypocrite
    d) Honest

4. According to Chanakya, what is the best way to gain knowledge?

    a) By self-study
    b) By serving the knowledgeable
    c) By attending debates
    d) By practising rituals

5. What is the primary duty of a student, as per Chanakya?

    a) Earning money
    b) Serving society
    c) Acquiring knowledge
    d) Gaining popularity

Section 2: Ethics and Morality

6. Which quality does Chanakya say is more valuable than beauty?

   a) Humility
   b) Wisdom
   c) Patience
   d) Generosity

7. According to Chanakya, a man is judged by:

   a) His wealth
   b) His education
   c) His behaviour
   d) His connections

8. What is Chanakya's view on helping others?

   a) Help only those who can repay
   b) Help without expecting anything in return
   c) Avoid helping anyone
   d) Help only close family

9. Which of the following actions does Chanakya discourage?

   a) Speaking truthfully
   b) Keeping secrets
   c) Gambling
   d) Being ambitious

10. What does Chanakya suggest about anger?

    a) It is a sign of strength
    b) It destroys wisdom
    c) It should be expressed freely
    d) It makes one respected

Section 3: Wealth and Prosperity

11. According to Chanakya, what is the true wealth of a person?

    a) Gold
    b) Family
    c) Knowledge
    d) Power

12. What is the recommended way to save wealth, according to Chanakya?

    a) Hoarding it
    b) Spending on luxuries
    c) Investing wisely
    d) Lending to friends

13. Chanakya says that wealth earned dishonestly:

    a) Increases quickly
    b) Is short-lived
    c) Is respected
    d) Brings happiness

14. What does Chanakya recommend doing in times of financial difficulty?

    a) Borrow money
    b) Seek advice from the wealthy
    c) Prioritise savings
    d) Sell Property

15. What should one avoid while spending money, as per Chanakya?

    a) Donations
    b) Excessive luxury
    c) Family needs
    d) Investments

Section 4: Leadership and Governance

16. What does Chanakya suggest is the foremost duty of a leader?

    a) To ensure justice
    b) To accumulate wealth
    c) To build alliances
    d) To maintain secrecy

17. According to Chanakya, how should a leader deal with enemies?

    a) Forgive them
    b) Ignore them
    c) Crush them strategically
    d) Make them allies

18. What is a key trait of a successful leader, as per Chanakya?

    a) Charisma
    b) Resourcefulness
    c) Physical strength
    d) Popularity

19. Chanakya advises leaders to:

    a) Trust everyone
    b) Trust no one
    c) Trust but verify
    d) Depend on allies

20. What type of governance does Chanakya advocate?

    a) Dictatorial
    b) Democratic
    c) Benevolent autocracy
    d) Socialist

Section 5: Relationships and Alliances

21. How does Chanakya suggest identifying true friends?

    a) By their loyalty during adversity
    b) By their wealth
    c) By their flattery
    d) By their knowledge

22. What should one avoid in personal relationships, according to Chanakya?

    a) Honesty
    b) Dependency
    c) Forgiveness
    d) Mutual respect

23. What does Chanakya say about family disputes?

    a) They should be resolved publicly
    b) They should be resolved privately
    c) They should be ignored
    d) They should involve a mediator

24. How does Chanakya view alliances?

    a) They are unnecessary
    b) They should be based on trust
    c) They should be based on mutual benefit
    d) They should be long-term

25. What is the key to maintaining strong alliances, as per Chanakya?

a) Frequent communication
b) Mutual respect and understanding
c) Financial dependence
d) Shared enemies

Section 6: Strategy and Diplomacy

26. According to Chanakya, the key to successful diplomacy is:

a) Deception b) Open communication
c) Strategic planning d) Unconditional trust

27. What does Chanakya recommend regarding secrets in diplomacy?

a) Share them freely b) Keep them confidential
c) Use them to manipulate others d) Ignore them

28. As per Chanakya's strategy, How should one deal with enemies?

a) Befriend them b) Study their weaknesses
c) Confront them directly d) Ignore them

29. Chanakya suggests that treaties with other nations should be:

a) Based on mutual benefit b) Temporary
c) Avoided d) Unconditional

30. According to Chanakya, What is the first step in preparing for war?

a) Building alliances b) Strengthening the army
c) Weakening the enemy d) Gathering intelligence

Section 7: Personal Discipline

31. Chanakya emphasises that self-discipline leads to:

a) Wealth b) Wisdom
c) Respect d) All of the above

32. What does Chanakya recommend as a daily habit?

a) Meditation
b) Practicing humility
c) Reviewing one's goals
d) All of the above

33. According to Chanakya, the best way to overcome laziness is:

a) Self-motivation
b) External pressure
c) Financial incentives
d) Competition

34. How does Chanakya suggest dealing with temptations?

a) Avoid them
b) Indulge moderately
c) Resist them with determination
d) Seek help from others

35. Chanakya states that the foundation of success lies in:

a) Wealth
b) Physical strength
c) Discipline
d) Social connections

Section 8: Time Management and Productivity

36. According to Chanakya, the best use of time is:

a) Entertainment
b) Leisure
c) Learning and planning
d) Earning wealth

37. Chanakya advises avoiding which habit of saving time.

a) Gossiping
b) Networking
c) Reading books
d) Practicing rituals

38. How does Chanakya view procrastination?

a) As a minor flaw
b) As a destroyer of success
c) As a natural trait
d) As a sign of creativity

39. According to Chanakya, What is the ideal way to manage multiple tasks?

a) Prioritise based on urgency
b) Delegate everything
c) Avoid multitasking
d) Finish the easiest tasks first

40. Chanakya recommends starting the day by:

    a) Checking finances
    b) Meditating and planning
    c) Socialising
    d) Completing household chores

Section 9: Karma and Destiny

41. Chanakya suggests that karma:

    a) Is irrelevant to success
    b) Defines one's destiny
    c) Can be ignored
    d) Is controlled by others

42. What does Chanakya say about good deeds?

    a) They bring immediate results
    b) They accumulate over time
    c) They are often unnoticed
    d) They are unnecessary

43. How does Chanakya view hard work?

    a) It is secondary to talent
    b) It is essential for success
    c) It often goes unrewarded
    d) It should be avoided

44. What does Chanakya advise about relying on destiny alone?

    a) Accept it fully
    b) Combine it with effort
    c) Reject it completely
    d) Depend on others

45. According to Chanakya, how should one react to failures?

    a) Give up
    b) Blame others
    c) Learn and adapt
    d) Ignore them

Section 10: Contentment and Ethics

46. Chanakya states that true happiness lies in:

    a) Wealth
    b) Contentment
    c) Power
    d) Fame

47. What does Chanakya suggest about ethical behaviour?

a) It is optional
b) It is the foundation of respect
c) It is a weakness
d) It hinders success

48. How should one handle ethical dilemmas, according to Chanakya?

a) Follow personal interest
b) Prioritise honesty and fairness
c) Seek external validation
d) Avoid decision-making

49. Chanakya's advice on contentment emphasises

a) Avoiding ambition,
b) Being satisfied with necessities,
c) Accumulating wealth
d) Competing with others.

50. What does Chanakya say about greed?

a) It motivates success
b) It leads to ruin
c) It is unavoidable
d) It enhances relationships

.

1	C	2	B	3	C	4	B	5	C	6	B
7	C	8	b	9	C	10	B	11	C	12	C
13	B	14	C	15	B	16	A	17	C	18	B
19	C	20	C	21	A	22	B	23	B	24	C
25	B	26	C	27	B	28	B	29	A	30	d
31	D	32	D	33	A	34	C	35	C	36	C
37	A	38	B	39	A	40	B	41	B	42	B
43	B	44	B	45	B	46	C	47	B	48	B
49	B	50	B								

Long Answer Questions

1. Explain the relevance of Chanakya's teachings on governance in modern-day politics.

2. Discuss Chanakya's advice on the importance of education and its impact on personal development.

3. How does Chanakya Niti address the concept of morality in wealth accumulation?

4. Illustrate Chanakya's leadership principles with examples from historical or modern leaders.

5. Analyse Chanakya's perspective on selecting the right friends and allies.

6. Describe the qualities of an ideal king as per Chanakya and how they apply to modern-day CEOs.

7. Discuss the role of self-discipline in achieving success, according to Chanakya Niti.

8. What does Chanakya say about anger and how it impacts decision-making?

9. Examine Chanakya's advice on secrecy and its importance in personal and professional life.

10. Compare Chanakya's teachings on justice with contemporary judicial systems.

11. How does Chanakya Niti emphasise the significance of time management?

12. Discuss the importance of strategic planning in Chanakya's philosophy.

13. What does Chanakya say about balancing personal and professional life?

14. Explain the role of women in Chanakya's philosophy and its implications in today's context.

15. How does Chanakya Niti guide individuals in dealing with failures?

16. Analyse the relevance of Chanakya's teachings on diplomacy in international relations.

17. Discuss the importance of contentment as per Chanakya's teachings.

18. What are the key lessons on wealth management derived from Chanakya Niti?

19. How does Chanakya Niti address the concept of karma and its role in shaping destiny?

20. Evaluate Chanakya's perspective on the role of ethics in leadership

Selected Quotes of Chanakya

Chanakya, the ancient Indian scholar, teacher, and strategist, left a treasure trove of wisdom behind. His teachings, deeply rooted in practicality and foresight, inspire leaders, thinkers, and individuals seeking personal and professional growth. Here is a selection of Chanakya's most profound quotes, along with insights into their relevance:

On Leadership and Governance

1. **"A person should not be too honest. Straight trees are cut first, and honest people are screwed first."**

   Insight: Chanakya emphasises the importance of balancing honesty with practicality in leadership and decision-making. Blind honesty can make one vulnerable in a competitive world.

2. **"The king shall lose no time when the opportunity waited for arrives."**

   Insight: This underlines the importance of decisiveness and acting swiftly when circumstances align favourably.

3. **"The welfare of the people is the ultimate law."**

   Insight: True leadership prioritises the well-being of the people over personal gain or power.

4. **"An insecure ruler tends to oppress his subjects."**

   Insight: Stability and self-confidence in leadership are crucial for fostering trust and harmony in governance.

5. **"A weak ruler is the cause of a nation's downfall."**

Insight: Strength and capability in leadership ensure a nation's prosperity and security.

On Wealth and Financial Wisdom

6. **"Before you start any work, always ask yourself three questions: Why am I doing it, what the results might be, and will I be successful? Only when you think deeply and find satisfactory answers, go ahead."**

   Insight: Planning and foresight are essential for financial success and decision-making.

7. **"Wealth, if not attained properly, will surely perish."**

   Insight: Ethical means of earning and managing wealth lead to lasting prosperity.

8. **"Accumulated wealth is saved by spending wisely, and knowledge is protected by constant application."**

   Insight: Effective resource management ensures sustainability.

9. **"Savings are the foundation of financial independence."**

   Insight: Chanakya underscores the importance of discipline and prudent saving.

10. **"A determined and industrious man can turn poverty into prosperity."**

    Insight: Hard work and determination are keys to financial success.

On Knowledge and Education

11. **"Education is the best friend. An educated person is respected everywhere. Education beats the beauty and the youth."**

    Insight: Knowledge is an enduring asset that opens doors and commands respect in every field.

12. **"A man is born alone and dies alone, and he experiences the good and bad consequences of his karma alone, and he goes alone to hell or the Supreme abode. Therefore, a man should act**

rightly."

Insight: Personal responsibility and ethical conduct are fundamental to a meaningful life.

13. **"Even if a snake is not poisonous, it should pretend to be venomous."**

    Insight: Projecting strength and confidence is essential, even when one feels vulnerable.

14. **"An uneducated man is like a blind person walking along the river's edge."**

    Insight: Education provides clarity, direction, and safety in life's journey.

15. **"Knowledge increases by sharing, not by saving."**

    Insight: Generosity in sharing wisdom enriches both the giver and the receiver.

On Relationships and Social Dynamics

16. **"Never share your secrets with anybody. It will destroy you."**

    Insight: Discretion is crucial in maintaining personal and professional relationships.

17. **"Learn from the mistakes of others. You can't live long enough to make them all yourself."**

    Insight: Observing and learning from others' experiences can save time and avoid unnecessary failures.

18. **"He who is overly attached to his family members experiences fear and sorrow, for the root of all grief is attachment."**

    Insight: Balance attachment with detachment to avoid emotional suffering.

19. **"Avoid the company of wicked people, as one avoids a poisoned dish."**

Insight: The influence of negative people can lead to one's downfall.

20. **"Friendship is tested in times of adversity."**

    Insight: True friends reveal their loyalty during difficult times.

On Resilience and Perseverance

21. **"As soon as the fear approaches near, attack and destroy it."**

    Insight: Courage and proactive action are key to overcoming fear and challenges.

22. **"A man is great not because he hasn't fallen, but because he rises every time he falls."**

    Insight: Resilience and learning from failures define true greatness.

23. **"There is no austerity equal to a balanced mind, and no happiness equal to contentment."**

    Insight: Inner peace and a balanced mindset are the ultimate sources of strength and happiness.

24. **"Success comes to those who act, not those who merely dream."**

    Insight: Action and persistence are essential for achieving goals.

On Strategic Thinking

25. **"He who is overly ambitious often sacrifices the essentials for temporary gains."**

    Insight: Strategic planning requires balancing ambition with practicality.

26. **"Test a servant while in the discharge of his duty, a relative in difficulty, a friend in adversity, and a wife in misfortune."**

    Insight: True character is revealed in challenging times.

27. **"One who controls the mind is more powerful than a king."**

    Insight: Self-control and discipline are more incredible power sources than external authority.

28. **"It is the responsibility of a wise person to turn a weakness into a strength."**

    Insight: Adaptability and strategic thinking are vital for success.

29. **"In the happiness of his subjects lies the king's happiness; in their welfare lies his welfare."**

    Insight: Leadership thrives when focused on collective well-being.

Summary

Chanakya's quotes encapsulate profound wisdom that is as relevant today as it was in his time. His teachings inspire us to lead with integrity, plan with foresight, and act courageously. By internalising these lessons, we can navigate life's complexities and strive for success and fulfilment in all aspects of life.

Recommended Reading on Chanakya and Ancient Indian Philosophy

Exploring the wisdom of Chanakya and the broader spectrum of ancient Indian philosophy can provide profound insights into leadership, governance, ethics, and personal growth. The following is a curated list of books and resources that delve into Chanakya's teachings and the philosophical underpinnings of ancient India:

Books on Chanakya

1. **Arthashastra by Chanakya (Kautilya)**
    - **Description:** A seminal work on economics, statecraft, and military strategy, the Arthashastra is a foundational text that offers insights into governance, administration, and policy-making. Translations by scholars like R. Shama Sastry are widely regarded.
2. **Chanakya Neeti**
    - **Description:** A collection of aphorisms and life lessons attributed to Chanakya. The text emphasises ethics, diplomacy, and practical wisdom for everyday life and leadership.
3. **Chanakya: The Kingmaker and the Philosopher by Anu Kumar**
    - **Description:** This book offers a narrative of Chanakya's life, focusing on his role in establishing the Maurya Empire and his enduring legacy.

4. **Corporate Chanakya by Radhakrishnan Pillai**
    - **Description:** A modern take on Chanakya's principles, this book adapts his teachings for corporate leadership, strategy, and personal development.
5. **Chanakya in You by Radhakrishnan Pillai**
    - **Description:** A motivational guide blends storytelling with Chanakya's teachings to inspire readers to achieve their goals.
6. **The Legend of Chanakya by Ashok K. Banker**
    - **Description:** A historical fiction novel reimagines Chanakya's journey and the challenges he overcame to shape the Maurya Empire.

Books on Ancient Indian Philosophy

7. **The Upanishads** (Various Authors)
    - **Description:** These ancient texts explore metaphysical questions, self-realisation, and the nature of the universe. They are foundational to Indian philosophy.
8. **The Bhagavad Gita**
    - **Description:** A timeless dialogue between Arjuna and Krishna, this text offers guidance on ethics, duty, and the path to self-fulfilment.
9. **The Vedas** (Rigveda, Samaveda, Yajurveda, Atharvaveda)
    - **Description:** These ancient scriptures form the cornerstone of Indian philosophy and spirituality, addressing rituals, hymns, and cosmic knowledge.
10. **Indian Philosophy by Sarvepalli Radhakrishnan**
    - **Description:** A comprehensive overview of the schools of Indian philosophy, this work delves into concepts like Vedanta, Buddhism, and Jainism.

-

11. **The Essentials of Indian Philosophy by M. Hiriyanna**
    - **Description:** This accessible text introduces the major schools of thought in Indian philosophy, including Nyaya, Mimamsa, and Samkhya.
12. **Nyaya-Sutras by Gautama**
    - **Description:** A foundational text of the Nyaya school, focusing on logic, epistemology, and debate.

Modern Interpretations and Applications

13. **Being Different by Rajiv Malhotra**
    - **Description:** This book explores the uniqueness of Indian philosophy and its relevance in the global context.
14. **India Unbound by Gurcharan Das**
    - **Description:** A modern narrative connecting ancient Indian philosophy with contemporary economic and social progress.
15. **Why I Am a Hindu by Shashi Tharoor**
    - **Description:** A reflection on Hindu philosophy, ethics, and its application in modern life, touching upon ancient texts and practices.

Online Resources

- **Stanford Encyclopaedia of Philosophy**: Offers detailed articles on Indian philosophical traditions, including Vedanta and Buddhism.
- **Kautilya's Arthashastra (Online Translations)**: Access various translations and interpretations of the Arthashastra for deeper study.
- **MOOCs and Online Courses**: Platforms like Coursera and edX offer courses on Indian philosophy and Chanakya's teachings.

How to Approach These Texts

1. **Start with Context:** To understand the broader themes, begin with introductory books like Chanakya Neeti or The Essentials of Indian Philosophy.
2. **Explore Core Texts:** For deeper insights, move on to foundational texts like the Arthashastra and the Bhagavad Gita.
3. **Apply the Learnings:** Use modern interpretations like Corporate Chanakya to integrate ancient wisdom into daily life and professional settings.
4. **Reflect and Discuss:** Join forums, book clubs, or online discussions to share perspectives and expand your understanding.

By immersing yourself in these recommended readings, you can unlock the timeless wisdom of Chanakya and ancient Indian philosophy, gaining insights that are as relevant today as they were centuries ago.

www.ingramcontent.com/pod-product-compliance
Lightning Source LLC
Chambersburg PA
CBHW062140160726
48282CB00027B/888
* 9 7 8 9 3 3 4 1 9 9 4 1 3 *